LING-NAM

The Reverend Dr. Benjamin Couch Henry was born in 1850 near Sharpsburg, Pennsylvania. In November 1873 he set sail for China. He was a missionary, an educator and a scholar who also enjoyed writing up his travels and sketching, as well as engaging in numerous speaking tours. Henry often addressed very large audiences across the United States to raise money for the American Presbyterian Church's China Mission during his furloughs home from China where he was largely based in Canton (Guangzhou). *LING-NAM* was first published in 1886.

Paul French, who has introduced and annotated this reprint, was born in London and lived and worked in Shanghai for many years. His book *Midnight in Peking* was a *New York Times* bestseller and a BBC Radio 4 Book of the Week.

LING-NAM

Hong Kong, Canton and Hainan Island in the 1880s

By Benjamin Couch
"BC" Henry
(1886)

Annotated by Paul French

BLACKSMITH BOOKS

China Revisited: No. 3 of a series

Ling-Nam

ISBN 978-988-75547-7-6

Published by Blacksmith Books
Unit 26, 19/F, Block B, Wah Lok Industrial Centre,
37-41 Shan Mei Street, Fo Tan, Hong Kong
Tel: (+852) 2877 7899
www.blacksmithbooks.com

Foreword and introduction copyright © 2023 Paul French

Cover photo: Shops and signboards in 雙門底 (Sheung
Mun Tai Street), Guangzhou. Photograph by A Chan (Ya Zhen).
Image courtesy of Special Collections, University of Bristol
Library (www.hpcbristol.net). Many thanks to Jamie Carstairs
and Robert Bickers of the Historical Photographs of China
project at the University of Bristol.

CONTENTS

ABOUT CHINA REVISITED

China Revisited is a series of extracted reprints of mid-nineteenth to early-twentieth century Western impressions of Hong Kong, Macao and China. The series comprises excerpts from travelogues or memoirs written by missionaries, diplomats, military personnel, journalists, tourists and temporary sojourners. They came to China from Europe or the United States, some to work or to serve the interests of their country, others out of curiosity. Each excerpt is fully annotated to best provide relevant explications of Hong Kong, Macao and China at the time, to illuminate encounters with historically interesting characters or notable events.

Given the prejudices of the era, what are we to take from these works? Some have a stated agenda, namely colonial control and administration of Hong Kong and Macao, or else proselytising and saving souls for the Christian religion. This is generally obvious in the writing. Others have no stated objective but impressions of the regions, their peoples, and cultures are products of their time and value systems. There is an unsurprising tendency to exoticize, make generally unfavourable comparisons to their home cultures and societies, and to misunderstand what they are witnessing.

They are – whether from American or European sources – invariably from men and women of some formal education. Their acquaintances are among the colonial authorities and foreign diplomats. These "filters" mean that invariably we are given an elite view of China; this is not the experience of the non-officer class sailor, merchant seaman, regular soldier, or working-class visitor. Even before we get to racial prejudice we are encountering class prejudice.

The writers in this series were all men and women of their time, encountering China at specific times in its history. Most of them were visitors or residents for a limited amount of time. However, some, notably the missionaries, did remain for longer – decades in some cases. In general the only foreigners who had credible local language skills were the missionaries, or British colonial district officers and their Portuguese equivalents in Macao, along with some diplomat-scholars. Assumptions were made, prejudices voiced, yet all of these writings have something to reveal of the encounters from which they derived.

FOREWORD

"South of the Ridge"

The Reverend Dr. Benjamin Couch Henry's *LING-NAM: Interior Views of Southern China (Including Explorations in the Hitherto Untraversed Island of Hainan)* was published by SW Partridge & Co of London's Paternoster Row in 1886. Henry was a missionary, an educator and a scholar who also enjoyed writing up his travels and sketching, as well as engaging in numerous speaking tours. Henry often addressed very large audiences across the United States to raise money for the American Presbyterian Church's China Mission during his furloughs home from China where he was largely based in Canton (Guangzhou).

The bulk of Henry's working life was spent in and around Canton. The term "Ling-nam" is little used now but was more current in the late nineteenth century. "Ling" means mountain in Cantonese, while "nam" means south, and the phrase is a shortcut for an important mountain range in the region. When people said "Ling nam", it also invariably meant they were going to Canton.

The chapters of *LING-NAM* concerning Henry's brief description of Hong Kong, and especially his detailed 'walking tour' of Canton, as well as his descriptions of the outlying towns of the Pearl River Delta are a detailed literary snapshot of the region in the 1880s and so therefore, despite his sometimes rather overtly missionary tone (and therefore almost total disregard for traditional southern Chinese religions and belief systems), are worthy of republishing.

Additionally, Henry claimed that his expeditions to Hainan Island had been the most extensive by any foreigner to date. Indeed, Henry referred to the island as the 'hitherto untraversed island', an only partially true claim. However, his expeditions were certainly the most extensive undertaken to date by a foreigner when he initially embarked on them in October and November 1882. Therefore, this volume includes a section of Henry's narrative concerning his journey and experiences on Hainan.

Henry's journeys through the silk, tea and market garden regions of the Pearl River Delta are of interest and rarely discussed in such detail by foreign observers. However, it should be noted that Henry's renderings of small town and village names in Chapter III – *Through the Delta* is effectively indecipherable and relating them to current locations is problematic.

INTRODUCTION

The Reverend BC Henry's Southern China Tours

B enjamin Couch ('BC') Henry was born in 1850 near Sharpsburg, Pennsylvania. His older brother Joseph fought with the Union Army during the American Civil War. He attended Princeton University and Seminary.

Having been raised in the Presbyterian faith, Henry was ardently religious from a young age. He became a Doctor of Divinity (DD) in 1870 at just twenty years of age. In November 1873 he set sail for China to become a missionary with the American Presbyterian Board of Missions (APBM), stationed initially at Canton. He would remain in China until 1894, a little over twenty years' service. In 1892 Henry was appointed the President of the Lingnan Presbyterian University for two years.[1]

---

1   The university moved to Macao in 1900 due to the Boxer Uprising, back to Guangzhou in 1904 and then to Hong Kong in 1938 after Guangzhou fell to the Japanese army. After World War Two the university moved back to Guangzhou and then finally in 1952 was merged with Sun Yat Sen University

He married and had three children, all born in Canton – Helen (1879), Morris (1886), and Edna (1893). As President of the university, Henry's despatches were regularly included in the annual report of the Board of Home Missions of the Presbyterian Church.

As well as acting as a missionary and an educator Henry was also an assiduous plant collector across southern China, concentrating on Kwangtung (Guangdong) Province, and also collecting on the island of Hainan. His fascination with the flora and fauna of Hong Kong and southern China are obvious throughout the pages of *LING-NAM*. Henry went on collection trips with his wife, the first to Hainan believed to be in 1882. The couple were good friends with Henry Hance, a British diplomat who had arrived in Hong Kong in 1844 and later become Consul to Canton and then Amoy (Xiamen). Hance devoted all his spare time to the study of Chinese plants and taxonomically categorised many Chinese species with help from the Henrys. Hance named a plant after Henry – *Rhododendron henryi* (Henry's Red), which has its native range in southern China and on the island of Taiwan. *The Colfax Chronicle* newspaper of Louisiana

in Guangdong while an alternative Lingnan University was founded in Hong Kong as a public liberal arts institution.

claimed that Henry was the first 'white man to collect insects on that island for scientific purposes.'[2]

***

Henry's first book was *The Cross and the Dragon: Or, Light in the Broad East*, published in 1885, a rather overtly Presbyterian tome that focuses on the deeply unwelcoming reception in China of Western Protestant missionaries in the 1870s.[3] This volume was followed swiftly by *LING-NAM*, which despite some religious exclusionary language and ideas is much more of a useful travelogue than generic missionary screed. *LING-NAM* is essentially a culmination of Henry's travels and time living in Hong Kong and southern China. He also spent two months travelling around Hainan Island, the interior of which was at the time little known to westerners. Henry also recounts the story of the initial Roman Catholic missionaries who had visited Hainan and who had all but completely disappeared by the time Henry explored the island. He was also a keen anthropologist interested in the island's various ethnic groups, such as the Lois, as well as the various languages and dialects of Hainan.

---

2   'Mimicry in Nature', *The Colfax Chronicle*, January 27, 1887, p.2.

3   BC Henry, *The Cross and the Dragon: Or, Light in the Broad East* (New York: DF Randolph and Company, 1885).

Though in *LING-NAM* a walk through the streets, markets, temples and alleyways of Canton is described in detail as if it is a single journey, it is clearly a composite of Henry's many walks through the city as a missionary. Indeed, at one point Henry notes, '…an audience of perhaps two hundred people are listening to an American missionary, who, speaking with fluency and animation, is holding their attention while he expounds the doctrines of Christianity.' It is easy to imagine that Henry has decided to write himself into the story here.

***

The late 1880s and early 1890s, just after the writing and publication of *LING-NAM*, became a harder time for Henry and for all foreigners (especially Christian missionaries) in southern China. He experienced the anti-foreign riots of 1891 and believed China to perhaps be on the brink of all-out rebellion. In a letter to the Navy Department in Washington DC, published in the *Fall River Globe* newspaper of Fall River, Massachusetts, Henry wrote of '…a feeling of uneasiness throughout the kingdom and that rioting in northern and central China are spreading to southern China and Canton.'[4]

4　'Navy Department in Receipt of Chinese Advices', *Fall River Globe*, August 19, 1891, p.1.

Things would get yet still worse for Henry. Though resident in Canton, Henry was responsible for a range of American Presbyterian Church properties across southern China as a trustee of Lingnan University, and on the board of various missionary-associated educational institutions across Guangdong province. In 1894 anger boiled over at Shek Lung, in Hong Kong's New Territories district, and a mission-funded school, overseen by Henry, was burnt to the ground and one 'native Christian' killed.[5] Disease outbreaks had led the British colonial authorities in Hong Kong to burn the houses of victims, not unsurprisingly angering many who eventually retaliated against this harsh practice. Henry wrote to say that rumours were flying around Hong Kong and southern China that foreigners were vivisecting living Chinese men and women for medical purposes.[6] Although in 1885 Henry appealed to the Presbyterian Friends of Christian Education in China for funds to establish a Christian College at Canton, he eventually decided to leave China for good later the same year.

---

5   Shek Lung (Stone Dragon) is probably a small village that existed in the Ting Kau area in the Tsuen Wan district of the New Territories.

6   Henry quoted in 'Fanaticism in China: Disorder Caused by Government Attempt to Stamp Out Plague', *Harrisburg Daily Independent*, August 1, 1894, p.2.

BC Henry died in June 1901 at the New Jersey State Hospital for the Insane at Morris Plains, New Jersey.[7] He was aged just fifty. His gravestone, at Greensburg Cemetery in Sharpsburg in Pennsylvania, describes him as:

"Rev. BC Henry, DD, of Canton China."

---

7   Now the Trenton Psychiatric Hospital, a state-run mental hospital located in Trenton and Ewing, New Jersey.

LING-NAM

(This text and spelling taken from *LING-NAM: Interior Views of Southern China Including Explorations in the Hitherto Untraversed Islands of Hainan, Chapters I, II, III & XVII*, by BC Henry, London: SW Partridge & Co., 1886)

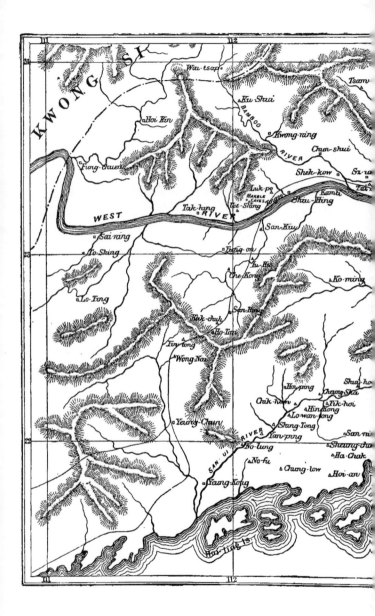

MAP
OF
CENTRAL CANTON.

Explanation of Signs.
Cities   ◻
Market Centres.   △

VICTORIA HARBOUR, HONG-KONG.

CHAPTER I

THE ENTRANCE TO CANTON

Hong-kong harbour and city – Botanical gardens – The Peak – Pidgin English – Up the Pearl River – Approach to the city – Throngs of boats – First impressions of a Chinese city – A busy people…[8]

The traveller from the east or from the west usually receives his first impression of southern China from the charming and picturesque island of Hong-kong. Entering the harbour of Hong-kong in the early morning, its quiet, lake-like beauty impressed one favourably, as it lies almost land-encircled between the Victoria Peak and the high hills on the mainland opposite. Its waters, usually placid, but often stirred into wild confusion by the dreaded typhoon and other storms, are well covered with a busy and animated maritime life. Steamers from all parts of the world come and go incessantly, bearing a rich

---

8   Spelling of Hong Kong as alternatively Hong-kong and Hongkong were common up until the early 1950s.

and varied commerce. Sailing-ships from Oregon, New York, Norway, or Australia, bringing cargoes of timber, kerosene, and other goods that admit of long transit, and taking matting, rattan, and similar articles in return, lie in the outer circle. Grotesque junks from the north coast of China, on their semi-annual trips, and an almost endless line of motley craft peculiar to a Chinese port, from the clumsy red-sided, dragon-eyed passenger barge, to the little mat-covered sampan, fill in the details of the scene.

Beyond this thronging life on the water rises the city, beautiful for situation and tastefully laid out. Skirting the shore are the long streets, the Praya and Queen's Road, along with the principal streams of traffic flow.[9] Merchant houses of fine proportions and most comfortable appointment, and the extensive barracks for the British troops, occupy its central portion, while the inferior structures of the Chinese *hongs* stretch far to the east and west.[10] The streets rise one above the other in terraces far up the slopes. Many of the residences are of palatial

9   Hong Kong once had the Praya Central, a stretch of seafront that fell victim to reclamation in the late nineteenth century though the use of the term Praya (or sometimes Praia) to describe the waterfront continued until the Second World War and even beyond among older Hong Kong residents.

10   *Hong* – originally a type of Chinese merchant intermediary in Canton (Guangzhou), latterly the term for any trading company based in Hong Kong, Macao, or Canton.

dimensions, surrounded by ornamental grounds filled with tropical plants that flourish luxuriantly. Roads high up on the hillside have been constructed at great expense, and extend for miles east and west, affording facilities for most attractive walks and short excursions in Sedan chairs.

Government House occupies a conspicuous site, overlooking the harbour and town beneath, and is surrounded by broad parks and gardens.[11] Many sheltered roads lead to the upper parts of the town, shaded by evergreen arches, which the interlacing branches of the ever-present banyan have woven. Profusely flowering creepers and tree-ferns of wondrous size and grace overhang the walls and line the walks that lead up ravines, where art has assisted nature, not only in confining the wayward mountain brook to its rock bound channel, but in bringing more plants to mingle with the native beauties. These, with opportune seats in secluded nooks, offer cool retreats from the heat of a tropical sun.

Among the chief attractions of the island we place the Botanical Gardens, where an unusual number and

---

11 Government House, on Government Hill in Central, designed by Charles St George Cleverly, was constructed between 1851-1855 in the Colonial Renaissance style. Its first occupant was the Governor Sir John Bowring (1854-1859). The building was altered significantly by the Japanese during the Second World War.

variety of rare and beautiful plants flourish in great luxuriance under the assiduous and efficient care of those in charge.[12]

It is less than half a century since Hong-kong came into the possession of Great Britain, and, although it then appeared to be but a barren, uninhabited rock, it has proved unusually rich in floral treasures.[13] The work of afforestation has been actively carried forward, hundreds of thousands of young trees having been planted over the hills, and the native growth of the island protected from the depredations of Chinese wood-cutters. As a result of this work, the rocky hills are becoming gradually clothed with trees, and the island fast assuming the appearance described by travellers centuries ago when its well-wooded slopes and profusion of fragrant flowers attracted their attention, and made the name Hong-kong – "Fragrant Harbour" – one of real poetic import, and no mere fancy. In the family of ferns alone one hundred and twenty species are enumerated as being indigenous to the island, besides the many that have been introduced from abroad and successfully cultivated.

Above the botanical gardens rises the peak, reached by a well-constructed footpath, up which strong coolies bear

12   The Hong Kong Zoological and Botanical Gardens were founded in 1864 and initially opened to the public in 1871.

13   1842 to be precise.

Sedan chairs with comparative ease. Besides the main peak, on which the signal station stands, are several others of lesser height, on the slopes of which are many houses and cottages highly prized by the citizens as summer residences.[14] These peaks, which lie fully open to the strong sea breeze, have become a popular resort, and all the land available for building purposes has been bought up, while the construction of roads in all directions has brought the isolated peaks into easy communication with each other and the town below.

But Hong-kong is not Canton, and the phases of life shown among the Chinese there are modifications, more or less divergent, of the real life seen in the middle kingdom itself. The houses they live in, their modes of doing business, and even their social life, are widely different from the same things under the rule of the mandarin.

The peculiar jargon of "Pidgin English", so widely used, greets the ear as something at once harsh and ludicrous, as we hear such expressions as the following: "My wantchee you catchee chow-chow chop-chop," to which the reply comes, "Man-man my waitee dat coolie come back, he belong one piece fulo man too muchee chin-chin joss," or the following in a silk shop: "More better you cum shaw

---

14   The "signal station" referred to being the Victoria Peak Signal Station.

my one piece, sillik numba one look see," to which the shop-keeper objects, "No can my make too muchee losee, you no like, maskee, my chin-chin you come back."

Leaving Hong-kong by one of the very comfortable steamers that traverse the Pearl River to the provincial capital[15], we pass through a succession of attractive river scenes, until we reach the narrow pass of Fu-mun, or Tiger Gate, otherwise known as the Bogue.[16] Military stations rise on either side, all fresh and white from recent repairs, with guns, banners, and heaps of ammunition, together with some thousands of soldiers, which show the importance attached to the place as one to be held at all hazards against invading forces. Beside the land fortifications are several gunboats and a supply of torpedoes, ready to be placed in the channel should necessity require. Their estimate of the importance of this pass, which commands the entrance of the whole broad expanse of Canton waters, is not exaggerated; and if their skill in fortification and use of the means of defence were equal to the occasion, they could hold it against almost any force. Above the Bogue the river is still very wide, and is bordered by broad fields of rice and extensive banana plantations, with high mountains in the distance. The

15 Of Kwangtung, or Guangdong, province.
16 The *Bocca Tigris*, derived from the Portuguese *Boca do Tigre* (Tiger's Mouth).

"lotus-flower" pagoda stands on a lofty hill opposite the mouth of the East River, so placed as to throw back over the land the good influences which the strong current of the river would otherwise carry to the coast.

The steamer calls at Whampoa, once the anchorage for ocean ships and the site of a busy trade, but which, since the opening of Canton as a treaty port, has sunk into insignificance, being almost forgotten in the rush of traffic between Canton and Hong-kong.[17]

Two fine specimens of pagodas appear on the left as we proceed, and abreast the second are extensive fortifications on the island in the river and the mainland as well. Passing these, the towers of the "City of Rams"[18] begin to appear distinctly, the French cathedral rising conspicuous over all, both for its size and for the beauty

---

17 Whampoa being romanised commonly now as Huangpu and Whampoa Island as Pazhou Island.

18 The "City of Rams" alternative name for Guangzhou derives from the Five Genii (or Immortals) Taoist temple. The myth goes that at one time, Sun Hao made Teng Xiu a governor but, before reaching his prefecture, there were five immortals riding five coloured sheep and bearing the five grains who came upon him and, after he received them, they left. Now the prefectural hall's beams bear the five immortals riding five coloured sheep for good luck. There are other versions of the story, though all involve five sheep or rams in one form or another.

of its architecture.[19] We are soon in the midst of the boats that densely line the river on both sides for a distance of six miles, backed in some places by rows of wooden huts, set on piles above the slimy mud of the tidal river. Scores of immense black barges are used as warehouses for salt, the sale of which is a Government monopoly, while similar vessels farther up receive cargoes of grain brought in for temporary storage. Junks, cargo-boats, floating-stores, and a dozen varieties of passenger barges, with innumerable smaller craft, swarm on all sides, or lie packed in solid phalanxes across the stream. A score of gunboats, of various sizes, well equipped with the most recent improvements in gunnery, show the naval armament of the city, to which should be added a hundred or more war junks, brave in their display of bunting, the name of each commander emblazoned in letters a foot or more square in the centre of a large triangular flag. Drifting slowly by a large collection of flower-boats, gay with lamps and mirrors, and richly furnished with black-wood sofas and embroidered curtains, in the scenes of nightly revelries, where the richer youth of the city indulge their passion for feasting and debauch, the steamer pulls up to the wharf. Dire confusion is often created among the slipper-boats, whose anchorage adjoins, by the surging

19   The Cathedral of the Sacred Heart of Jesus, also known as the "Stone House" locally.

of the steamer against their outer lines, causing them to jump, and sputter, and dart about like a swarm of ants, shell-like craft, whilst they vociferously hurl maledictions at the great steamer.[20]

At first sight the whole city seems one mass of low houses, with here and there a square tower rising above its humbler neighbours, the narrow streets being scarcely discernible as we pass up the river. From the breezy deck and comparative quiet of the steamer we are suddenly transported into the midst of the hot atmosphere and seething masses of humanity that crowd the wharf and press through the narrow streets. It takes but a moment to realise that we are in China. Every sense is assaulted and overwhelmed with proof that we are in the midst of a people of strange speech and peculiar habits. It seems an effort to breathe, and the wonder to us is that people can live in such pent-up quarters. This feeling, ere long, wears off in a measure, and we soon become accustomed to streets but eight or ten feet wide; become indifferent to the crowd of curious gazers constantly at our back; display admirable fortitude in the presence of sights and smells that were staggering at first, and are fully absorbed in all the new, strange phases of life presented in the streets. Everyone seems busy and good-natured. The rush of coolies with their burdens; the whir of the jade-cutting wheels; the din

20 "Slipper boats" being wooden pleasure craft.

of the brass founders, the clang of the forge, the clatter of the silk loom, worked by hand; the monotonous thud of the goldbeater's hammer, the patient stitching of the embroiderers, under whose skilful fingers grow patterns of wondrous beauty; the markets, with hurrying throngs bringing in fruits of every variety, vegetables, and live fish; and the thousand other employments carried on in shops opening full on the street, impress us strongly with the fact of their great industry.

CHAPTER II

"THE CITY OF RAMS"

The missionary hospital – Female seminary – Pawnshop – Dog and cat restaurant – Swatow Guildhall – Ivory and sandalwood carving – French cathedral – Jade-stone Street – Funeral procession – Execution ground – The Emperor's temple – New Year's ceremonies – Modes of greeting – Examination Hall – Viceroy and train – Preaching Hall – The Double Gate – Temple of Horrors – The five-storey tower – Goddess of Mercy – The city wall – Sleeping Buddha – Tartar quarter – Flowery pagoda – English consulate – Mosque – Temple of the Five Genii – Prison – Bribery – Ebony furniture – Signs – Curio Street – Silk shops – Native hospital – Houses of the rich – Honam – Buddhist temple – Shameen – Flower gardens – Floating down the river…

In order to see the city to advantage some central point should be chosen from which to make excursions; we therefore select, as the most convenient point of departure, the group of mission houses on the river's bank a short distance below the steamer's wharf.

There we see the great hospital which for nearly half a century has been a fountain of benevolence to the suffering Chinese. Founded by Dr. Parker[21], it has for the past thirty years been under the efficient care of Dr. Kerr, who, besides being a surgeon of extraordinary skill and success, is also one of the most devoted and self-denying men the world has ever seen.[22] The annual attendance of patients is from 16,000 to 24,000, and the number of surgical operations performed is from 1,000 to 1,200 every year. A large class of medical students, including three women, now under instruction, give promise of the spread of true medical science in the south of China.

21　Peter Parker (1804-1888) was an American physician and missionary. He arrived in Canton in 1834 and opened the Ophthalmic Hospital (later the Boji Hospital). Parker left China in 1857.

22　John Glasgow Kerr (1824–1901), an American who helped establish the Canton Hospital, also known as the Ophthalmic Hospital. Kerr arrived in Canton in 1854 with his wife to run the Huiji Dispensary of the Presbyterian Mission and the Canton Hospital and remained for 45 years. In 1859, Kerr opened Boji Hospital, located in southern Canton and served as a superintendent of the Canton Hospital from 1855 to 1898. In 1860, Kerr opened the second dispensary in Foshan, later becoming the largest hospital in the city. In 1899, Kerr opened the first mental hospital in China.

Across the street is the female seminary, with one hundred and forty pupils. It has been brought to a high degree of efficiency under the superior management of Miss Noyes, and is proving a source of light and knowledge to the women of the land.[23] These institutions are indicative of the future, and deserve a closer study than we can give them in the rapid glance bestowed.

Sedan chairs borne by coolies are in waiting to bear us through the maze of narrow streets, which in their labyrinthine character are utterly bewildering to the stranger. A few steps bring us to the front of one of the square towers observed from the river. It is a pawnshop, where money is advanced on clothing and valuables at high rates of interest, and where people can deposit articles for safe keeping. Ascending the narrow winding stairs, rows of packages, each labelled carefully, fill the tiers of shelves. The rates of interest are usurious, and the pawnbroker is the virtual possessor of all that comes into his hand.

Regaining the street, we come, after two sharp turns, face to face with eating-houses, where the peculiar shape of the articles exposed for sale attracts attention. Closer inspection shows them to be dogs, the tip of the tail or

23   Ohio-born Martha Noyes (1840-1926), employed by the Presbyterian Board of Missions. Noyes married John Kerr in 1886.

the foot attached leaving no room for doubt, while the whole body of a puppy freshly dressed and ready for the kettle is held up by the grinning attendant. A covered pot nearby displays a card, on which are these enticing words, "Pure, sweet, black cat always on hand inside," and lifting the wooden lid, a collection of what might be cat, rabbit, or something else for aught we know, is seen.

After a few more turns through dingy, crooked streets we come to the hall and temple of the Swatow Guild, a magnificent structure with highly-carved pillars and richly ornamented cornices and ceilings.[24] It is an assembly hall for the merchants of Chin-chow, where they meet to transact business.[25] A certain idol is chosen as their patron, to which regular worship is paid, while once a year a series of theatrical performances are given in the rear court, where a pavilion, with a permanent stage, is erected in front of the main reception-hall. This reception-room, called the "Hall of the Southern Pearl," sparkles with mirrors and chandeliers and vases of antique porcelain, while the walls are decorated with curiously written scrolls and ancient drawings. The temple was erected at a cost of two hundred thousand dollars, and

---

24 Representing the merchants of what is now Shantou, Guangdong province.

25 Qinzhou, Guangxi province.

is now receiving an addition that will almost double the original size.

Entering the city through the Oil Gate, we pass tubs of live fish offered for sales, and are borne through the tinware street, past the shops where ivory and sandal-wood carvers are busily engaged with their little knives, chisels, and files turning out articles that find their way to every land, until we come to the French cathedral. Occupying a most desirable location, on the site of the official residence of the famous Viceroy Ye, with several acres of ground, it excites the envy, and not unfrequently the hostility, of the populace.[26] The ground was obtained in restitution for property destroyed in the interior many years ago, but the people believe it to have been wrested unjustly from the Government. The cathedral itself is a fine Gothic structure, built of granite, and will compare favourably in size and proportions with many of the renowned churches of Europe.[27] It rises above every other building in the city, its tower spires showing conspicuously

---

26 Hubei-born Viceroy Ye Mingchen (1807-1859), a high-ranking Chinese official noted for his resistance to British influence in Canton following the First Opium War. During the Second Opium War Ye was arrested by the British in Canton and, in violation of diplomatic procedure, was transported as a prisoner-of-war to Fort William in Calcutta where he died a year later. His remains were later returned to China for burial.

27 The cathedral is Gothic Revival style technically.

for many a league. It is not simply the spirit of arrogance which they trace in so lofty a structure, but the omen of ill luck which their theory of geomancy shows it to be, that leads them to regard it with the greatest disfavour, and has made it necessary to station guards of soldiers for months at a time to protect it.

Leaving this finest piece of architecture in the south of China, our course leads us through the streets of the rich jade-stone shops, where various ornaments in every shade of green are displayed in the greatest profusion, and where the tastes and purses of all can be suited from a pair of earrings for fifty cents up to bracelets for three thousand dollars. Curio shops, with unique collections of rare porcelain, bronze, or ivory, invite our inspection.

Passing the barn-like offices of several petty mandarins, near which are rows of shops, where bows of various strength, with arrows and all that is necessary for the outfit of a military contestant are supplied, we find the street obstructed by a funeral procession. In advance of the coffin, which is borne by four stout coolies, runs a man with rolls of white paper cut in the form of coins, which he scatters along the street. This is to buy up the way, that the spirits may not annoy the soul of the dead as it passes with the coffin. Behind the coffin staggers a man clothed in sackcloth, his head bound with a white turban, supported by two attendants, who hold a bowl before his face to catch his tears, while he loudly laments the misfortune that has bereaved him of his father. The procession must take a circuitous route outside the city wall to reach the place of the burial, as no corpse is allowed to enter the city.

Diverging from the main street to escape the ill-luck of following a coffin, our coolies bring us to the execution ground, a triangular piece of land where criminals are beheaded. The wretches are carried hither in baskets, and, bound hand and foot, are placed in kneeling posture, while the executioner, if he be skilful, severs each head at a blow. A sword so used is considered an object of great interest, and even clergymen have been known to purchase such bloody mementoes of the place. It is a veritable potters' field, the space being used, in the interval between executions, as the drying-ground for the pottery works adjoining.

Re-entering the city, we pass the arsenal, where guns are cast and munitions of war prepared under the superintendence of men trained in western methods, and soon find ourselves in the open court before the Emperor's Temple called the "Man-Shau-Kungi," or "Palace of Ten Thousand Ages."[28] It consists of a series of halls, one

28   The Emperor's Temple is described as follows in *A Pictorial Handbook to Canton*: 'The Emperor's Temple was built in the early part of the eighteenth century. It is situated in the same

behind the other, built of wood painted red, with dragons in white outlined over the surface, and roofed with tiles of imperial yellow. No image of any sort appears within, only a large gilt tablet, on which are inscribed the words, "May the Emperor live ten thousand years, ten thousand times ten thousand years." Worship is here offered by the officials alone, on New Year's morning and on the Emperor's birthday, and special mourning rites performed at stated times on the occasion of the death of certain members of the royal family. The New Year's ceremonies are by far the most conspicuous and important. At that time every official in the city, from the lowest to the highest, must pay homage before the imperial tablet. The gates of the city are open all night long to facilitate the arrival of the mandarins. The lowest in rank goes first, so that the highest may have someone to receive him, and sends word to the next above him that he has started, and after a certain interval he sets out, sending a similar message to his superior. In this way they gather, those below a certain rank – that is, from the Prefect downward – remaining in the court in front, while the Tao-tais and

---

street as the Viceroy's Literary Club. On certain days during the year all Civil and Military mandarins are obliged to come here to worship the Imperial Tablets of the Emperor and Empress.'
Source: *A Pictorial Handbook to Canton* (Middlesbrough: Hood & Co., 1905), p.11.

all above them assemble in the entrance hall.[29] The civil mandarins are received on the east side of the pavilion and the military on the west. They come in their robes of state to the number of a hundred or more, and, it being winter, are usually clothed in the richest of sables. Each has his attendants, who bring cushions for him to sit upon, and a trunk containing citizens' clothing, so that he may be ready, should sudden news come of his removal from office, to adopt immediately the ordinary dress. It is interesting to watch their modes of greeting. As the civil mandarins come in, the first three or four greet each other on equal terms, each bowing low, with clasped hands. As those higher in rank appear, they greet the lower in groups of twos or threes, the Happo, or Superintendent of Customs, always a member of the royal family, giving one general bow to all, while the Viceroy responds to the low obeisance of the whole company with a horizontal stare, standing erect with his hands folded before his chest.[30] The military kneel in squads as the Tartar general, their chief, comes in, while he responds by hurried bows

29   A Tao-tai (or Taotai) being a high provincial officer, who has control over all civil and military affairs of a *tao*, or circuit, containing two or more *fu*, or departments, the officers of which are accountable to him.

30   The Happo (sic), or more commonly Hoppo, was the term for the Administrator of the Canton Customs, the official at Canton with responsibility for controlling shipping, collecting

as he hastens along the line. When all have assembled and daylight approaches, they proceed in a body to the second court, and face the open door of the hall where the tablet is seen. A crier is stationed, who calls the postures in a deep, sonorous voice, saying, "Kneel," and they fall on their knees; "Bow the head," and all bend over; "Prostrate yourselves," and they fall on their faces; "Arise," and they all stand up. The order and number of these bows and prostrations are regulated by law. No form of prayer is offered.

Entering the old city through the "Gate of Literary Brightness,"[31] we come to the great hall of examinations, where the candidates for literary honours once in three years compete for the degree of A.M.[32] They come to the number of twelve thousand or more, and are shut up in cells, six feet by three, for twenty-four hours at a stretch, while they write essays, odes, and historical disquisitions on subjects selected from the old classics. About one in each hundred succeeds in leaping the Dragon Gate, as the usual metaphor expresses it.

---

tariffs, and maintaining order among traders in and around the Pearl River Delta. The post existed between 1685 and 1904.

31   Looking at photographs from the period it seems that the aforementioned Viceroy's Literary Club also functioned as a gateway. The Literary Club appears to have been a place where the Viceroy of Canton often entertained visitors.

32   Henry means a Master of Arts degree.

Proceeding thence, we pass the largest Confucian temple in the province attached to the Prefectural College, and the great temple of the God of War, and reach the street leading from the Great South Gate to the office of the Provincial Treasury.[33] The cries of a courier to clear the street for the procession causes us to stand aside, and soon a small cavalcade on ponies with jingling bells appears, coolies carrying present boxes, others with banners and great gongs, while behind them, in a chair of state borne by eight coolies in uniform, sits a portly mandarin; his satin robes, with embroidered breast-piece, hat with a red button and peacock's feather, are noted as he passes. It is His Excellence the Viceroy on his way to pay official calls. The rear is brought up by a motley assortment of half-grown boys and men in red coats, tall wire hats, bearing pikes, flags, and numerous red panels, with the honours bestowed on his excellency inscribed.

This temporary obstruction creates a dense crowd in the street, to escape which we enter a mission chapel, where an audience of perhaps two hundred people are listening to an American missionary, who, speaking with fluency and animation, is holding their attention while he expounds the doctrines of Christianity.

33 The Great South Gate is also known as the Ta-Nam Mun, Tae-nan Mun or Tai-naam Moon. The only city gate that remained open at night.

Under the double gate we pass one of the oldest structures in the city, dating back to the fourth or fifth century, stopping for a few moments to examine the water clock in the tower over the gate, which has been measuring time by drops for several centuries.

Entering the crowded thoroughfare that bisects the city in a line from the east to the west gate, we soon come to the city Palladium, often called the "Temple of Horrors," where idolatry in its most rampant form is always to be seen.[34] About the doors are throngs of beggars, most persistent in their claims for the wealth-giving cash, while inside are itinerant traders, tinkers, dentists, herb-doctors, jugglers, fortune-tellers, sweet meat-traders, gamblers, and a perfect babel of noise and disorder. On either side, in separate stalls, are fine representations of the Buddhist hell, where the most hideous physical tortures are depicted, and at the main shrine is a throng of worshippers, men, women, and children, prostrating themselves. Delicate ladies, who ordinarily would scarcely venture to a neighbour's house, are here pushed and jostled in the crowd as they seek some boon from the patron deity. Clouds of incense and smoke from burning paper and candles, combined with the heat, suffocate us, while the din of the incessant explosion of fire-crackers

---

34 It seems Henry is here referring to the Shing Wang Temple, sometimes known as the City Temple.

is most deafening. This temple is leased by the Prefect to a company at a rent varying from $4,000 to $7,000 a year, this rent, and the fortune expected in addition, being made from the proceeds of worship.

From this point we strike through less crowded portions of the city, and reach the Five-Storey Tower on the north wall, from which an unobstructed view of the city and surrounding countryside is obtained. This height was occupied as early as the first century of our era by Chin-t'oh, the first Prince of Uet.[35] The present tower, constructed some three hundred years ago, is called the "Sea Guarding Tower," and is supposed to control the geomantic influences in such a way as to bring peace and prosperity to the city.[36] Tea and refreshments of the native sort may be had while the visitor studies in detail the variations of mountain, plain, city, and river presented in the wide scene before him, and enjoys the cool breezes that ever play around these heights. In close proximity, on an adjoining hill, cluster the courts and temples of the Goddess of Mercy.[37] Up the steep flights of steps leading to this shrine devotees daily toil to receive the help of the

---

35   Qin Shi Huangdi, First Emperor of China.

36   The Zhenhai Tower, also known as the Five-Storey Pagoda, the Sea Guardian Tower is located in Yuexiu Park, Guangzhou. It was completed in 1380.

37   Kwan Yin, or Guanyin.

many-handed goddess, whose attributes of "great in pity, great in compassion, saving from misery, saving from woe, ever regarding the cries that come up from the world," find a deep response in the hearts of the multitudes of this people, sunk in misery and wretchedness such as few of us can know. Ignorantly they worship a creature of the imagination, but in so doing show the groping of hearts conscious of their need of sympathy and help which the Redeemer of men only can give.

The wall of the city, along which we now travel, is built of sandstone, and has stood the ravages of war and time for more than a thousand years. In the interstices of the stone and brick, hanging like folds of graceful drapery, are found many beautiful clusters of maiden-hair fern (*Adiantum flabellatum*). We pass over the North Gate, and onward to the north-west corner of the city, where stands the oldest Buddhist temple in the south of China. Among other objects of interest we are shown a sleeping Buddha, the Knowledge Tree (*Ficus religiosa*), brought from India by Tat-mo, the great apostle of Buddhism in China[38], and an iron pagoda, under which is enshrined the hair of the sixth patriarch, who underwent tonsure at

---

38 Tat-mo was a monk from India who travelled to China to spread Buddhism.

the foot of the sacred tree.[39] The place has a dilapidated air, and a shaven monk, bearing a fish in his hands, is not a very striking example of strict adherence to a vegetable diet. A stroll through the Tartar quarter reveals a people of darker colour, larger and more bony frames, and of a somewhat different dress from the Chinese. The women appear with three brass rings in each ear, and sky-blue robes that reach to their feet. These people form the permanent garrison of the city, and receive a Government allowance, in consideration of which they hold themselves in readiness to answer any call for service. Their part of the city shows a marked contrast to the purely Chinese portion. Their houses are smaller and poorer, and an air of neglect, thriftlessness, and decay spreads over all.

Near the office of the Tartar general rises, in stately proportions, the "Flowery Pagoda," a wonderful structure nearly two hundred feet high, built thirteen hundred years ago, and recently repaired at public expense of $40,000.[40]

---

39 Dajian Huineng, also commonly known as the Sixth Patriarch or Sixth Ancestor of Chan, is a semi-legendary but central figure in the early history of Chinese Chan Buddhism. According to tradition he was an uneducated layman who suddenly attained awakening upon hearing the Diamond Sutra.

40 The Flower Pagoda, also known as the Flowery Pagoda, is part of the Temple of Six Banyan Trees. The pagoda was in a poor state of disrepair when Henry visited, with wild plants

Across the narrow street are the grounds of the English consulate, formerly a part of the Tartar general's residence to vindicate the perpetual right of the English to enter at will, and live, if so disposed, within the city walls. Gardens, pleasure grounds, a park with deer, and a line of houses in Chinese style, with apartments furnished with European comfort, where the Duke of Edinburgh and other distinguished visitors have been entertained, make it an attractive place. The tower of the "Smooth Pagoda" next invites us, and entering the enclosure at its base, we come upon a Mohammedan mosque, and learn that this peculiar pagoda, unlike in shape to any other of Chinese origin, was built by the early followers of the false prophet, who extended their conquests to the east in the seventh century.[41] It was used for centuries as a minaret, from which the hours of prayer were called, but has fallen into decay, so that no one dares ascend to its top. Inquiring of the teacher whose little school adjoins the entrance-hall, we learn that in Canton there are five hundred families

growing from its different storeys. It was significantly restored in 1900.

41   The Flower Pagoda's counterpart was the minaret, located in the Huaisheng Mosque, or Tower of Light. It was first built in 850 and reconstructed in 1468, and is still standing today. It was given the nickname of "Smooth Pagoda". The minaret is proof of an Arab presence in Guangzhou since the Tang dynasty.

who hold the faith of Mahomet, and are introduced to a portly individual with a jovial countenance, who tells us he has performed a pilgrimage to Mecca.

The next point of interest is the Temple of the Five Genii, one of the most remarkable structures in the city.[42] It derives its name from the legend of the founding of the city in which it is related that five genii, riding upon five rams, with clusters of the five cereals in their hands, appeared to the inhabitants of the place, and presenting to them the grain, with the wish that they might prosper and multiply, suddenly disappeared. The rams were changed into stone on the spot, and, so the story runs, are preserved to this day, five rough pieces of rock being exhibited as the identical stones into which the rams were transformed. From this remarkable occurrence Canton is popularly called the "City of Rams," and also the "City of the Genii." This temple, with its numerous courts, is a concrete epitome of Chinese worship, all the principal deities, to the number of a score or more, being represented. The great object of interest, however, is the tabooed bell which hangs silently in its massive tower. No hand dare strike it, and when, at the dictates of fate, its tones are heard, disaster is sure to follow. This superstition is confirmed by several remarkable occurrences. On one

---

42 The Taoist Temple of the Five Immortals, formerly translated as the Temple of the Five Genii.

occasion the beam on which it was suspended gave way, and the bell fell with a crash; forthwith plague and famine desolated the city. Again, when repairing the tower, a workman accidentally struck it with his hammer, and a pestilence broke out that swept off young children in great numbers.

In the last war with China, when the British troops held the heights north of the city, the legend of the tabooed bell was brought to mind, as aiming at prominent buildings, a cannon shot struck it, breaking a piece out of its side.[43] The city capitulated soon after, many believing the bell to have sounded its doom. The broken bell still hangs in its tower, an object of wonder and dread to the credulous people, who know not the day when its ominous peals may be heard again.

Leaving the Tartar quarter, we make our way to the office of the Nam-hoi magistrate, where justice is supposed to be administered. As we approach, the street is lined with prisoners, with stones chained to their legs or necks, or broad wooden collars, called *cangues*, intercepting communication with the head. Some are making shoes, some sewing, others twisting rope, but

---

43   Henry is referring to the Second Opium War, also known as the Second Anglo-Chinese War, the Second China War, the Arrow War, or the Anglo-French expedition to China (1856-1860).

all are dirty, unkempt, ill-fed, wretched-looking objects. Passing into the inner prison, where squalor and misery appear supreme, hordes of gaunt, ragged, hairy objects gather around us, begging for money, each with a piteous tale of wrong. Some are not able to rise, still suffering from the effects of the bastinado, or with their knees raw from kneeling on broken glass or chains, or with their ankles crushed by wooden hammers. The aim of the whole course of treatment is to extract confession of guilt, and to this end torture is used unmercifully. The jailer receives no salary, and is compelled to furnish food to the prisoners, yet his position is a lucrative one. Whence the money comes we can but imagine, but the stories of hideous methods of torture used to extort it confirm our worst suspicions. No dignity appears in the court which we enter, and it is difficult to see how the ends of justice can be met, when no reliable means of collecting or sifting evidence are used. It usually becomes a question of which party can give the highest bribes, and the means to such unlawful gains open to the magistrate may be surmised from the fact that the incumbent of this office a few years ago, while holding his position but for ten months, made $180,000 in addition to his lawful income.

Returning to the main street, we pass out of the city through the "Gate of Virtue," and crossing a bridge over the city moat, we enter a street where black-wood furniture, richly carved and inlaid with marble and mother-of-pearl, forms the chief article of trade.[44] Chairs, tables, couches, stools, brackets, mirrors, and other articles are temptingly displayed. Beyond these are the furriers, and on the same street a row of shops where musical instruments are made, flutes, guitars, violins, etc., of the oddest shapes, a dozen varieties being offered for the modest sum of ten dollars. Passing these, long lines of shoe stores, with boots and shoes peculiar to the country, in all colours, displayed to catch the eye; marble shops, book stores, idol manufactories, incense shops, stores with silk thread of many hues, out-fitting establishments for theatres and processions; embroidery work in rooms open to the street, dozens of men, each with his own frame and pattern, stitching from morning till night, and many other interesting sights, are passed on our way to the Great Peace Gate, which leads us into the western suburbs of the city; medicine shops where ginseng, hartshorn, cassia, and a thousand other drugs, are sold; stores for hats and caps, umbrellas, spectacles, and fans are hurriedly seen, until we reach the banking street, where scores of shops with barricaded doors show shroffs busy over baskets of dollars, tying them up in gunny bags, or handing the doubtful coin to men who sit

---

44   The Gate of Virtue being the Kwai-tak-moon Gate or more commonly simply the South Gate.

in rows, with baskets of silver in sycee[45] or dollars, busily and deftly separating the true from the base.[46]

Beyond this we pass the large stores that deal in birds' nests, and offer this delicacy in quantities varying in price from fifty cents to several dollars an ounce. The remarkable combination of colour in the signs strikes us forcibly at this point; perpendicular boards, some thirty feet long and a foot wide, with the names of the shops and their business in large letters, green and gold, red and black, yellow, orange, blue, grey, and brown, painted, grained, or lacquered, form a perfect maze and wilderness of colours.

We are on our way to Curio Street, which no one fails to visit, where the richest of old porcelain is sometimes seen, *sang-du-boeuf* vases offered at $1,500 each, rhinoceros' horns, jade ornaments, and bronzes at fabulous prizes.[47] The silk shops form an attractive feature with all their rich display of fabrics woven by hand. Street after street is given up to this industry, the bright fabrics in wondrous colours and richness of texture growing slowly in the awkward looms which are manipulated by hands

---

45   Sycee is a form of silver money made in the form of ingots and formerly used in China.

46   The Great Peace Gate being alternatively the Tai-ping-moon Gate or simply the West Gate.

47   Curio Street is now Yuansheng Xijie Street.

and feet combined. The silk firms are mostly connected with some of the merchant houses, for whom they act both as agents and producers, often being under strict articles of agreement not to manufacture for or sell to any one but those so employing them. Before leaving the western suburbs we take a hurried look into the Wa-lam-tsz, "Flower Forest Monastery," a Buddhist institution of wealth and note, where in one hall are five hundred large gilded images, representing disciples of Buddha who have been deified.[48] Not far from this we are shown the ruins of one still more noted, the Temple of Longevity, which was destroyed a few years ago by an infuriated mob, excited to violence, it is said, by the immoral practices of the monks in charge.

In this vicinity, too, we find a native hospital and benevolent institution, called into existence as the rival of the missionary hospital, but doing a good work for the suffering, extending its charities to many points in the interior, where relief is given to people suffering from famine or flood, while it supplies coffins for all who die in indigent circumstances.

---

48   It is slightly confusing as to which temple Henry is referring to. He may be confusing the Flower Forest Monastery with the aforementioned Temple of the Five Genii, also sometimes referred to as the Wa-lam-tsz. Or he may mean the Buddhist Guangxiao Temple.

SCENE ON THE PEARL RIVER.

THE FRENCH CATHEDRAL, CANTON.

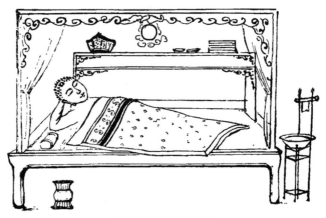

A SLEEPING BUDDHA.

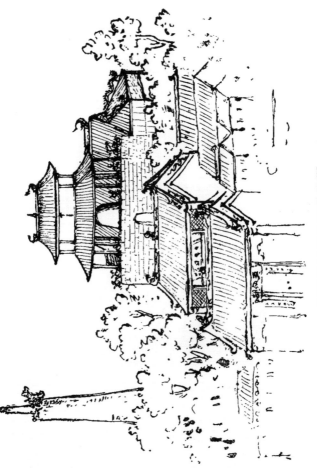

TEMPLE OF THE FIVE GENII.

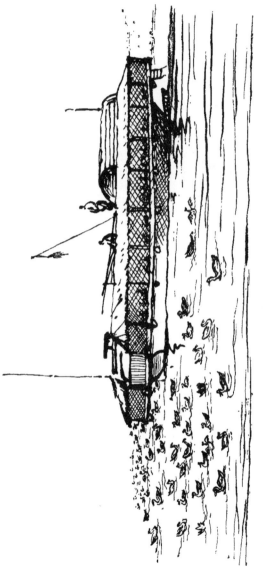

A DUCK BOAT.

58

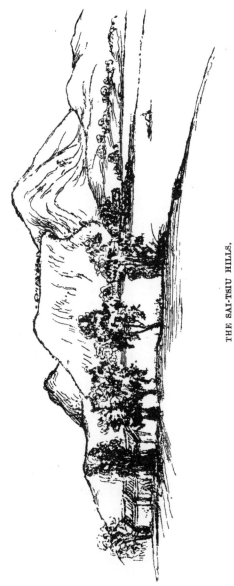

THE SAI-TSIU HILLS.

THE COCOA-NUT PALM.

In the western suburbs are the residences of many wealthy people, to which the stranger from other lands with a card of introduction may be admitted. The comfort of these houses is not evident, the only difference between them and the homes of the poorer people being in the material of which they are built, the general arrangements being much the same. Straight-backed chairs, with marble seats, stiffly arranged against the walls, sofas, and divans, whose hard polished surfaces glitter in elegance, but offer no ease, abound; beds, elaborately carved and adorned with silk and satin hangings profusely embroidered, but with only mats and porcelain pillows laid on the smooth boards, are not suggestive either of down or roses. Crossing the river on one of the many ferry boats, where the regular fare is two cash (one-tenth of a penny) – and the whole boat can be chartered for the trip for a cent – we reach the suburb of Honam, which, as its name indicates lies along the southern bank of the stream.[49] Furniture shops, tea *hongs*, and large matting manufactories occupy the chief place in its trade. Several streets are devoted to the work of porcelain painting, which is a delicate and interesting industry, requiring a good knowledge of colours and their properties to secure the right shades and combination after the ware has been submitted to the furnace.

---

49   Now the Haizhu District of Guangzhou.

The Great Buddhist Temple, covering several acres with its various halls and shrines, is worthy of a longer study than we can give it. The main hall, with its colossal images of the three precious Buddhas sitting on lotus flowers, is where the morning and evening liturgical services are performed, scores of shaven monks in yellow colashes joining in the repetitions. Sacred pigs and chickens, rescued from the vulgar fate of the butcher's knife, are cared for in a side apartment, until they die of old age, when they receive an honoured burial. Fruit and flower-gardens extend behind the buildings, and in a remote corner is seen the furnace in which the priests are cremated.

After this general view of the native city we are drawn irresistibly to the beautiful little island of Shameen, where most of the foreign residents live.[50] Formerly a mere sandbank in the stream, it has been surrounded by a strong wall, and elevated above the reach of the highest tides, and shut off from the native town by a canal spanned by two bridges. Elliptical in shape, and evergreen in its grass and foliage, it presents a perfect ideal of retirement and comfort. Park-avenue runs through the centre from east

50   Shameen, or alternatively Shamian, is a sandbank island in the Liwan District of Guangzhou that was controlled jointly by France and Great Britain at the time of Henry's visit.

to west, shaded by rows of noble banyans. The bund[51] on the riverside is the favourite promenade, being open to the south, whence it receives the full benefit of the refreshing south-east monsoon through the summer. The consulates, each with its ensign floating, the church with its bell and spire[52], the merchant houses, spacious, comfortable and richly furnished, the flower-gardens, tennis-lawns, and shady walks combine their varied interests and charms. To the south stretches the wide river, while men-of-war, coast steamers, and the yachts and pleasure boats of the community lie in the foreground. This charming spot was the scene of the furious mob in September of 1883, which in a few hours destroyed one-third of the houses, and changed the usual quietness into a reign of terror.[53]

Seated in a "matrimonial boat," one of the most spacious and comfortable used by the merchants, we row up the river to the flower-gardens in Fa-ti, where Chinese florists have exhausted their skill in twisting, stunting, and deforming plants, until a tree of more

---

51 Bund (rhyming with "shunned") being a Hindi word meaning a raised waterfront such as the more major ones found in Chinese treaty ports such as Wuhan and Shanghai.

52 Christ Church Shameen (Protestant), completed in 1865. A French Catholic church, the Our Lady of Lourdes Chapel, was completed after Henry's recounted visit, in 1892.

53 Due to heightened tensions between France and China that culminated in the Sino-French War (1884-1885).

than a century's growth still lives in a narrow pot, having never reached a height of more than three or four feet.[54] In their seasons many attractive plants are seen flowering in great abundance. Camellias, azaleas, chrysanthemums, euphorbias, magnolias, jasmines, lotuses, etc., attain great perfection in a climate where frost is a rare occurrence. Fruits for ornament are also much cultivated, and artistic arrangements of oranges, limes, loquats, citron, custard apples, lichees, and others are very effective. In these gardens arbours and pavilions erected over artificial ponds are suggestive of summer breezes, laden with the odours of sweet-smelling shrubs fanning the dreamy occupants, of broken sunlight dancing through the vines and lattice, and the murmur of the water fretting against the sides of the pond. Such romantic ideals, however, are seldom fulfilled in the midst of all the harsh commonplaceness that meets us even in these gardens, where nature struggles to be poetic in spite of her sordid tyrants, and in colours, aroma, and luxuriant leafage succeeds to a great degree.

Floating down the river by moonlight, when all is quiet and serene, when the hum of the busy hive has ceased and its myriads sunk to rest, with only the monotonous tone of the watchman, or the shrill cries of some industrious vendor of sweetmeats to break the stillness, with lights

---

54   Fati (or sometimes Fa-tee) – a suburb of Canton noted for its flower gardens.

from the shore and boats reflected in fairy-like radiance in the water, while the pale moon shed its pearly light over the sleeping city, our experiences of the day seem all a dream, a stupendous freak of the imagination. But the loud calls of our sturdy rowers, as they command the throng of boats to divide and open a passage for us to the landing, recall us to the world of reality, and the many strange scenes of the day commingling in all their varied forms and colours, are fixed indelibly upon the mind.

CHAPTER III

THROUGH THE DELTA

Extent of the Delta – White Goose Pool – Vapours of the "Dragon Well" – Teetotum Fort – Wong's Canal – The hills of Sam-shan – Admiral Keppel's exploit – The city of Fat-shan – Telegraph line – Glazed earthenware of Shek-wan – The rice district – Duck hatching – Duck boats – Network of streams – Sai-tsiu Hills – Cloudy Mist Tea – Grottoes and cascades – White Cloud Waterfall – Mulberry plantations – Plucking the leaves – Silkworms – Unwinding the silk – Character of the people in the silk district – Accident in a theatre – The women of Sai-tsiu – Anti-matrimonial league – Dense population – The town of Kow-kong – 300,000 men – Kom-chook rapids – Ku-lo and its tea – Down the broad West River – Pig's-Head Hill – Deep channel for steamers....

The delta of the Pearl River is one of the most remarkable in the world, in the richness of its soil, in the varied products it annually gives forth, and in the density of its population. Its apex is at Sam-shui (Three Rivers), the point where the West, North, and Pearl Rivers mingle their waters.[55] About fifty miles west of Canton its longest side runs south-east from that point, passing through the great cities of Fat-shan[56] and Canton, and ending in the Bay of Lintin, its whole length being about one hundred and forty miles.[57] The west side goes down from the same point in a straight line from north to south for two-thirds of its way, when a portion of the main stream of this West River is deflected, and flows through numerous creeks and canals, dissecting the lower portion of the San-ui district, which join their waters with a stream from the west, and pour into the sea through the Ngai-mun, the most westerly mouth of the delta. Leaving beautiful Shameen, with its massive bund and elliptical line of evergreen banyans, behind which are embowered the stately residences of the foreign community, we cross the little harbour called by the natives Pak-ngotam, "White Goose Pool."[58] On the right are seen the groves and cloisters of

---

55 Now a district of the city of Foshan in Guangdong province.

56 Now Foshan.

57 Now Nei (or Inner) Lingding Island in the Pearl River Estuary.

58 Pak-ngotam was a deep-water harbour and appears in many family histories and memoirs as a place of Chinese

the ancient Buddhist monastery Tai-tung, whose quiet courts and cool pavilions make it a popular resort for excursionists. Within the enclosure of the monastery is a well, remarkable, according to native accounts, for the vapours that were formerly said to have issued from it, presaging storms and tempests not only in the immediate vicinity, but at points remote in the interior and along the coast. A thick, lurid mist, it is said, issuing from some deep cavern, was wont to rise in volumes, covering the monastery and groves about, and ascending high into the air. These vapours are now said to appear in the well at certain times, but seldom extend beyond that narrow space. Accompanying the lurid mist, it is said that sounds like the cackling of geese are heard, leading to the belief that there is some subterranean connection between this well and the deep pool of Pak-ngotam adjacent. This pool, again, which is said to be in one place fathomless, is believed to be subterraneously connected with places as far north as Shiu-kwan[59], two hundred and eighty miles distant, as far west as Ko-chow[60], two hundred and fifty miles off, and far east as Chiu-chow[61], about the same

---

embarkation for new lives in Singapore and Southeast Asia in the nineteenth century.

59   Shaoguan in northern Guangdong province.

60   Gaozhou in southwestern Guangdong province.

61   Chaozhou in eastern Guangdong province.

distance. The well in which the mist appears is also called the "Dragon Well," and is supposed to presage storms, the "pulses of the earth" as these subterranean watercourses are called, bearing in advance the warning of their approach. The outward effect of these vapours is thus described by a native rhymester –

"When Tai-tung sends its clouds of mist afloat,
Each fishing craft appears a passage boat."

Three miles down the broad river we pass Teetotum Fort, which guards the approach to the city from the south.[62] It is strongly built, a pointed tower, or good-luck pagoda, rising in the centre, and giving it the appearance of the toy from which it receives its name. Traces of its occupation by the British are seen in the mottoes, proverbs, and names inscribed on its inner walls. It is built on a rocky islet, and on the banks adjacent several massive forts assist in the defence of this main waterway to the metropolis of the south.

To the right of this fort is the entrance to "Wong's Canal," which is passable for ordinary boats at high tide, and reduces the passage of six miles by the river to two. Its construction forms an interesting episode in Chinese annals. General Wong, an insurgent chief, was bearing

---

62 More commonly known as the Macao Fort Rock.

down upon Canton, and had reached the junction of the two streams a few miles below the site of the present fort, where a strong force was massed to oppose him. After a series of fruitless manoeuvres, he hit upon the plan of digging a canal across the low point of land between the two streams. Favoured by darkness, his soldiers worked with eagerness, and ere the fifth watch struck, had not only finished the canal, but had transported their boats through it to the main stream, whence, with the enemies behind, they pressed on to surprise the city by an early and unexpected attack.

This canal leads us into one of the main arteries that intersect the delta, called Fat-shan Creek.[63] On the right, as we ascend, the low rice lands are bordered by hills covered with tea plantations, and large villages set in shady groves. On the left is a series of hills called Sam-shan, which were formerly celebrated as one of the most attractive resorts near the city. The "clear dawn after rain," as seen from these hills, was considered one of the great sights of the time. They still preserve some of their former attractiveness, and are frequently visited on short excursions. In the centuries past, when covered with

---

63 Henry would have known Fatshan Creek by reputation as the site of one of the major engagements between the British Royal Navy and the Qing Imperial Navy in June 1857. After defeating the Chinese the British advanced upriver to Canton.

groves, the charm of the early morning after refreshing showers had quickened their manifold varieties of trees and plants into new life, may easily be imagined. The scene indicated is one of Nature's loveliest, appealing to the purest instincts of man's nature.

A short distance beyond the Sam-shan, we come to the scene of Admiral Keppel's famous exploit.[64] It was during the war of the allied forces against China, and the object of the special expedition then in hand to capture the great trading mart and manufacturing centre Fat-shan. The Chinese, aware of the approach of the British war vessel, had massed their whole naval force at one point. As the British drew near they saw a line of war junks stretched across the river with their guns trained to a certain point. Perceiving at once the weakness of their position, the admiral ordered his vessel forward under full pressure of steam, broke through the line of junks, receiving, as he passed, a simultaneous fire from all the junks, which, owing to the suddenness of the movement and inaccuracy of aim, fell harmlessly about the ship; and

---

64   Admiral of the Fleet Sir Henry Keppel (1809–1904) was a Royal Navy officer. He was commanding officer of the corvette HMS *Dido* on the East Indies and China Station and was deployed in operations during the First Opium War and in operations against Borneo pirates. At the Battle of Fatshan Creek he sunk a reported one hundred Chinese war-junks.

before the Chinese could recover from their surprise was speeding on toward the city.

Fat-shan is the second city in importance in the south of China, and 500,000 people are found in its compactly-built, closely-packed houses. Manufactories of various kinds abound, producing cloth, silk, embroidery, rattan and bamboo work, porcelain, brass, and ironwork. For the latter large cargoes of worn-out horseshoes and various forms of old iron are shipped from England. A large business is done in cassia, grain, oil, and timber. The city is intersected by two canals, which furnish the greatest facility for transport. The boat traffic between Canton and Fat-shan is immense. The proposition to run a small steamer over the fifteen miles between these two cities threatened to cause a mob, the tens of thousands of people dependent upon the boats for a living joining a general outcry, so that the project was given up. The telegraph line recently laid passes through Fat-shan, the general office being in the Wesleyan Mission Hospital.[65] Two attractive bungalows on the outskirts of the town, where missionaries reside, two flourishing churches under the direction of the London[66] and Wesleyan Missions,

---

65 The Wesleyan Methodist Missionary Society established at Fatshan (Foshan) in 1860.

66 Meaning the London Missionary Society.

and the hospital with its thousands of patients, show satisfactory progress in Christian and benevolent work.

On a bend of the stream a few miles to the south is the town of Shek-wan, famous in China for its glazed earthenware, seats, flower-stands, lattice-work, balustrades, flower-pots, tiles, animals, fruits, vases, plates, and ornaments in endless variation are produced.[67] This ware is very cheap but ornamental, the glazing being done in many colours, blue, green, white and red predominating. It is sometimes mistaken for the more costly porcelain, an instance of such confusion occurring in the New York Custom House a few years ago. A resident of Canton brought among other things two large flower-pots of this ware, which cost originally between four and five cents each. The owner's valuation was not accepted, and the articles were appraised at five dollars each.

From this point, looking south and south-east, we see stretching out the great rice-producing district, in the centre of which stands Chan-tsŭn, an important town with 100,000 people. A brisk trade with the ports on the sea coast is carried on, grain, salt-fish, and oil being the chief articles of commerce. This town was the port of Canton during the last war, when the city was under siege. The great rice plains of this district, partially submerged

---

67   Now the Shiwanzhen Subdistrict of Foshan and still producing Shiwan ware ceramics.

at high tide, are dotted with small hills and clumps of trees, which mark the sites of villages. Immense harvests are gathered continually, the land in some places yielding three good crops in a year.

These rice fields form the feeding for thousands of ducks, and the great lumbering boats – floating cages, in fact – in which they are conveyed from one point to another, are often striking features in the landscape. The ducks are hatched by artificial means, establishments for this purpose being found all over the country. The eggs are placed in baskets or wooden tubs, with chaff, bran, cotton, or fine grass between the layers. These baskets are set in rows in rooms heated to the proper temperature by charcoal furnaces. Daily attention is paid to the eggs, changing their position, testing the temperature, and other necessary precautions. When each brood of ducklings hatches out they are sent to market and sold. Many people devote their whole time to rearing ducks, and will have hundreds and thousands under their care. They keep them in boats of a peculiar shape made specially for the purpose. These odd-looking craft are pushed up and down the streams in search of good feeding grounds. Their favourite resorts are the paddy fields. Tying up beside the slender embankment that encloses the rice field, the duck-herd opens the door of his great cage, and his flock, clattering and quacking, rushes into the muddy field. Abundance of insects, worms, shell-fish, and crabs reward their search. After harvest the ducks come in as gleaners, and do their work thoroughly. They are under good discipline, and quickly respond to the calls of their keeper, following the boat as it moves along the stream. When evening comes a plank is put out and ducks called home. With a palm leaf brush on the end of a pole the keeper herds them in, the beating which the last one is sure to get causes great commotion among the last dozen. The keeper shouts and thrashes the tardy ones with his brush, causing them to rush pell-mell, each anxious to escape being the last.

The whole extent of this district is so intersected by canals, as to render every point easily accessible by water, and the incessant lines of boats of all shapes and sizes add life and variety to the scene.

> And gliding through the liquid maze
> A varied fleet is sped.
> With crystal net of waterways
> The teeming land is spread

The northern half of the western side of the delta is devoted to the cultivation of the mulberry shrub and the production of silk. As we enter the silk district, the most prominent object before us is the picturesque group of the

Sai-tsiu hills. These hills form a plateau of one thousand feet above the level of the sea, with seventy-two peaks of various heights rising up. The highest of these is the Tai-foh peak, from the top of which an unobstructed view of the richest and most populous district of south China is gained. Visitors to this peak frequently start from the town below at midnight, in order to reach the top in time to see the sun rise. A good paved road, lined with eleocarpus and liquid-amber trees, leads up the mountain side, through wooded glens, over bridges spanning deep ravines, beside cool grottoes and springs of delicious water. A large portion of the land among the hills is devoted to the cultivation of tea, the Wan-mo or "Cloudy Mist" tea from the Sai-tsiu hills having a great reputation among the Chinese.

Fourteen villages, of not less than a thousand people each, are found among these hills. Amidst the peaks are many gorges and cascades to delight the lover of nature, the most noted among them being the Tsui-ngam, "The Many-Hued Gorge," the Chŭ-hang, "Vermilion Ravine," and the Pák-wan, "White Cloud Cascade." Of all these charming spots Pák-wan is the most attractive. The great scholar Pak-wan had his study in this picturesque ravine, shaded by groves of fine trees, with the cool water ever pouring down the gorge. The cataract falls over the precipice above in a double stream, and flows out below under a natural bridge of stone. Half-way up is a small cave, reached with difficulty, before the opening of which the spray of the falling cascade hangs in a misty veil. Masses of delicate ferns, refreshed by continual moisture, hang richly over the walls, and within are stone seats on which to rest while listening to the music of the waters, and watching the sunlight break into rainbow colours through the falling spray. A native poet of some repute has described the scene in a couplet –

"Below the bridge, three streams their flows divided pour;
Above, the heavens are seen as through an open door."

Around the base of these hills, and for miles on all sides, the land is covered with mulberry plantations. The aggregate of many small interests go to make up this vast industry, and the division of labour affords employment for all ages and sexes. The mulberry shrubs are cut down in winter every year and used for fuel. The roots remain, and around them the soil is spaded and heavily fertilised. The surplus moisture is drained off into fish ponds, sunk deep in the midst of the fields. The young shoots sprout with the opening spring; and when the first crop of leaves is ready, usually in April, thousands of boys, women and girls are employed to strip them off, and pack them in baskets. Hundreds of men, in little boats propelled by paddles, dart back and forth along the canals, carrying these baskets of leaves to the market-places, where they are weighed by men detailed for that purpose, and purchased by the owners of silkworms. In some of the larger plantations cocooneries are found, but the silkworms are usually reared in the houses of the people in greater or less quantities, as they can afford. A crop of leaves matures every six weeks, in which time also a fresh brood of silkworms hatches out. The utmost yield of leaves is six crops in a year, the second and third, occurring in May and June, being considered the best. The mulberry leaves vary in price from twenty-five cents to one dollar and a half per hundredweight.

The silk cocoons, when ready to be unwound, are first plunged into hot water, and then set out to dry, after which the silk is unwound. Hundreds of women many be seen sitting by their doors winding the gossamer threads from the cocoons. The thread is hung up in dry, airy places, until all trace of moisture disappears. Sometimes, on clear, warm days, boats will be seen moving up and down the streams with rows of men and women winding off the silk, of which quantities will be suspended from frames along the top of the boat, that the wind blowing through may dry it. After this process it is ready for the market, and is bought up by companies and shipped to the centres of trade, a tax of one dollar per hundredweight being levied by the town corporation on all the raw silk exported from that district. In silk culture everything is done by hand, and everything is utilised. The refuse of the silkworms and cocoons is cast into the ponds to feed the fish, and the silkworm chrysalis, whose house has been appropriated, becomes an article of food, one of the delicacies of the season.

The people in the silk district are the most conceited, turbulent, and bitterly anti-foreign, and at the same time the most enterprising of all the people in south China. An attempt was made a few years ago to introduce machinery into one of the great silk establishments near Sai-tsiu, but the place was twice mobbed within a short time and the owners compelled to remove the machinery. The hills described are the great natural feature of the district, which brings, according to popular belief, good luck to the land, and the people look with jealous eyes upon the visits of "outside barbarians," who, professedly attracted by the charms of natural scenery, they suspect of coming to spy out and carry off the luck of the place. They have peopled the hills with spirits and deities of various kinds and degrees of power, and offer them constant worship. Beside these regular offerings to the presiding genii, special religious festivals are frequently held, in which theatrical performances play a prominent part. Their theatres are large square structures, composed of bamboo framework covered with matting and palm-leaf thatch. A gallery is set apart for ladies, and the women of Sai-tsiu show their independence by going in large numbers to the theatre. The performances are kept up day and night, and through their attempts to light the place with imperfect means at command accidents frequently happen. A frightful occurrence took place a few years ago in this district, in which a theatre capable of holding ten thousand people was destroyed by fire. The narrow entrance, and the dense crowds driven to desperation by their fear, made escape difficult so that no less than three thousand people, most of them women, perished in the flames. Despite such experiences the semi-religious performances in these theatres are still regarded as means of good luck to the place.

The high-spirited disposition of the Sai-tsiu women is shown in the organisation of an anti-matrimonial league, in which the fair damsels of this fortunate district bind themselves under solemn pledges never to marry. Such a course is so contrary to the whole history and spirit of Chinese institutions, and so daring a challenge to the practices of ages, that one cannot but admire the spirit of independence and courage from which it springs. The existence of the Amazonian league has long been known, but as to its rules and the number of its members no definite information has come to hand. It is composed of young widows and marriageable girls. Dark hints are given as to the methods used to escape matrimony. The sudden demise of betrothed husbands, or the abrupt ending of the newly-married husband's career, suggest unlawful means for dissolving the bonds. When they submit to marriage they still maintain their powers of will. It is a common saying that when a man marries a Sai-tsiu woman he must make up his mind to submit to her demands. The same characteristics are said to prevail among the women of Loong-kong, the next large town to the south, one of their demands being that the husband must go to the wife's home to live, or else live without her company.

No one who has not passed through this district can have any just conception of the density of the population. Besides innumerable villages, there are the great towns of Koon-shan, Sha-t'ow, Loong-kong, Loong-shan, Kow-kong, Lak-low, and Kom-chook, all lying close together.[68] Of these, Kow-kong is the largest, and forms a little kingdom in itself. It is said that during the war at the close of the Taiping rebellion, a census was taken with a

68 Kow-kong (in Cantonese) is probably today's city of Jiujiang (in Mandarin). Loong-kong would appear to be Longjiang and Ku Lo today's Gulao.

view to estimating the fighting strength of the people, and it was found that Kow-kong alone could furnish 300,000 able-bodied men as soldiers.[69] The limits of this town lie within a space five miles wide and seven or eight long. The town is composed of coteries of villages around the main centre of trade. They have one of the finest schools in the empire, the Ue-lam Shǔ-uen. Its students everywhere take high rank, and several of the leading gentry of the place have won the highest literary honours. The corporation controls all the town affairs, not allowing Government officials to have authority except in rare cases. Gambling, prostitution, and other evils are forbidden, and the laws, in most cases are rigidly enforced. It is said that a man may take his daughters to any place of entertainment in the town without exciting suspicious remarks. Their chief hatred, however, is against the foreigner, and they have sworn never to permit the hated barbarian to obtain a foothold in their town.

The tide of wickedness thrown back from the gates of Kow-kong finds ready admission through the open doors

69 The Taiping Rebellion, which is also known as the Taiping Civil War or the Taiping Revolution, was a massive rebellion or civil war that began in Guangxi province and was waged across much of China from 1850 to 1864 between the established Qing dynasty and the theocratic largely Hakka-led Taiping Heavenly Kingdom. Estimates of the dead from the conflict range from thirty to fifty million!

of Loong-kong, the adjoining town. There gambling and forms of vicious amusement flourish under the especial patronage of the gentry. The Kow-kong swarm the streets of the neighbouring town, and pour their money into the coffers of the Loong-kong people.

From the inner region of the silk district, the entrance to the main West River is over the Kom-chook rapids. When the tide is full it is an easy matter to cross these rapids, but when the water is down, a ledge of rock at the bottom causes the stream to rush and boil in an angry way. The choice then lies between engaging a dozen or twenty men, who are always waiting for a job, to pull the boat up by main strength, or make a *détour* of ten miles to the south by canal. A heavy stone wall protects the bank from erosion, and facing the rapids stands a temple to the Queen of Heaven, the patron goddess of sailors.[70] The boatmen always offer incense and wax tapers, sometimes fowls and pork, at this shrine to secure a safe passage.

Emerging from the narrow creeks and canals of the low-lying delta, the broad West River appears rolling down in stately volume. Its waters rise and fall with the tide, which checks, but cannot overcome, the strong current. Beyond its western bank to the north rise the Ku-lo Hills, covered

---

70 Mazu, also known as Matsu and Tin Hau, is a popular Taoist and Chinese Buddhist goddess. She is the goddess and patroness of the sea, believed to protect fishermen and sailors.

in places with a heavy growth of camphor trees, which are hewn and shipped to Canton to be made into boxes, chests, and furniture. Large plantations of the fragrant Ku-lo tea, so highly prized by the Chinese, cover the slopes of these hills, at the foot of which lies the town of Ku-lo with its opium-besotted people.

Sailing down the broad stream, a deep sense of peace comes over us as we lie dreaming on the upper deck, under the shadow of the grass-mat sail. Our reverie is broken by the captain asking if we want to buy a fish, and we descend to barter for a fine specimen of sam-lai, or Chinese shad, a fish of most exquisite flavour. A group of large grey cranes on the sandy beach attract attention as they stand, three or four feet high, lazily searching for shell-fish.

Before us, as we sail, rises the pyramidal form of Chŭ-t'ow-shan, "Pig's Head Hill," a rocky island crowned by a small watch tower. A guard boat marks it as a military post, and the remains of fortifications show its past uses, while on a hillside, on the shore opposite, is the grave of a company of braves, who fell in battle here. The broad West River is not always so placid as it seems in the day of early spring. Once during a stormy January, we made the journey up its stream, when its waves dashed high on the rocky shore. Long lines of men attached to the tracking-ropes, triple and quadruple the usual number, gave evidence of the force required to move the boat, while several dismasted boats and the wreck of a barge on the rocky head of Chŭ-t'ow-shan showed the force of a storm on its waters. Its channel is deep enough to admit steamers of the largest draught, but hitherto Government launches and small revenue cruisers are the only steam vessels that have traversed its waters. For two hundred and fifty miles it may be navigated by larger ships, and the city of Ng-chow (Wu-chow), within the borders of the province of Kwongsi, be brought into direct communication with the commercial world.[71] On our left, as we go down with the current, rise the towers and pagodas of many populous towns, while far to the east stretch the plains of Heung-shan, from which many emigrants have gone to the Hawaiian Islands.[72]

---

71 Wuzhou in Guangxi province.
72 Zhongshan in Guangdong province.

CHAPTER XVII

HAINAN, OR THE ISLAND OF PALMS

Terra incognita – Opening of the port of Hoi-how – Recent explorations – Hainan Straits – Red harbour – Exports from the island – Hainanese dialect – Surroundings of Hoi-how – Old Romanist cemetery – Missions in the past – The city of King-chow-fu – Cocoa-nut ware – Starting on our journey – Lives of coolies – Experience of opium-smoking – Black rock – Tribes of Aborigines become subject to the Chinese – The "Hummocks" – Extinct volcanoes – First night in an inn – Beef-eating – The city of Ching-mai – Wealth of vegetation – Sea-view Tower – Fine bridge...

Until very recently the great island of Hainan, lying just within the tropics, was an almost unknown land to the world outside; and the reputation it bore as the haunt of pirates and desperate characters did not encourage investigation. The streams of commerce swept past it, ships touching only when necessary at some of the better

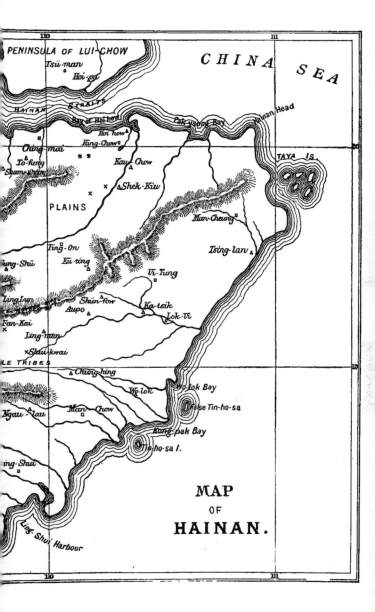

MAP

OF

HAINAN.

harbours, without coming into any direct relations with the people. When the opening of Hoi-how, the chief town on the island, as a treaty port was under discussion some fifteen years ago, public attention was for the first time directed toward it, and several gentlemen connected with the Chinese Customs and the English Consular service made the circuit of the island in gunboats, landing at several places, and penetrating a few miles inland.[73] One of them, the late Mr. Swinhoe,[74] made a journey of several days into the interior to the town of Ling-mun.[75] The information collected by these gentlemen gave many important facts in regard to the facilities for commerce along the coast, but contained nothing definite as to the natives of the country, the character, customs, and disposition of the people in the broad and as yet unexplored interior.

73　Hoi-how is the Cantonese pronunciation of Haikou, the capital city of Hainan province.

74　Calcutta-born Robert Swinhoe (1836-1877) was a British diplomat and naturalist who served at Amoy (Xiamen), acted as a translator during the Second Opium War (1856-1860) and was a consul at Formosa (Taiwan), Ningpo (Ningbo) and Chefoo (Yantai). An accomplished ornithologist, he discovered many species of birds across Southeast Asia and several were subsequently named after him. Swinhoe also served as a roving consul and it was in this capacity that he was instructed to visit Hainan.

75　A town in central Hainan.

Within the last few years Captain J Calder, in command of the Chinese gunboat *Sui-tsing*, has improved the exceptional opportunities afforded him of mingling with and observing the life and character of the aboriginal people of the south of the island.[76] His duties in the suppression of piracy and protection of the coast were such that he was not able to penetrate more than a few miles from the seashore; the extent of his observations, therefore, has of necessity been limited.

It was not until three years ago that the outside shell was really broken and the interior laid open. This was done in the first instance by Mr CC Jeremiassen, a Danish gentleman, who is now devoting himself, unaided, to independent missionary work for the people of the island.[77] In the months of April and May 1882

---

76 Captain James Calder was placed in command of the seized Imperial Chinese gunboat *Sui-tsing* in 1883. His duties included suppressing piracy along the southern Chinese coast and conducting a survey of the coast of Hainan which included a number of his own sketches.

77 The Reverend Carl Jeremiassen (1847-1901), a former sea captain who had worked on pirate suppression for the Qing dynasty-controlled Canton Customs Service. He visited Hainan a number of times, largely the south of the island. Though Danish-born, he became a missionary for the American Presbyterian Mission. He had completed a two-year apprenticeship in Canton Hospital and so was able to act as a medical missionary. Like Henry, Jeremiassen was something

he made the circuit of the island on foot, testing the practicability of travelling unmolested through every district, and proving the friendliness of the people. The detailed account of this first extensive journey made by a foreigner inland is replete with interest. During the past year he has crossed the island from north to south, and again from east to west, encountering no special hostility from the people in any part. In October and November 1882 it was my good fortune to make extensive journeys through the interior of the island with this gentleman, an account of which is subjoined.

Hainan forms the extreme southern limit of the Chinese Empire, being in itself one of the largest Prefectures of the Canton province, and lying, as it does, right abreast the Gulf of Tonquin, was threatened with invasion soon after the war in Tonquin brought the French into collision with the Chinese.[78] Raised from centuries of obscurity into sudden prominence by its position in relation to the contending parties, its size, its resources, its population,

---

of a linguist and completed the first translations of the Old and New Testaments into Hainan dialect. He later established a hospital at Haikou and managed to bring regular outbreaks of malaria on the island under control with the use of quinine. In 1901, Jeremiassen disappeared, rumoured by the Chinese on the island to be drowned in the sea though it appears more likely he died of typhoid.

78   Alternatively the Gulf of Tonkin.

its harbours, and general characteristics, became matters of eager inquiry. Called the "Island of Palms" by some, from the abundance of cocoa-nut palm, betel nut palm, caryota[79], fan palm, and date palm, it lies in a semi-tropical sea, and is one hundred and fifty miles in length and a hundred miles in breadth.

Our journey from Hong-kong to Hoi-how was made in a wretched little steamer, with the cabin immediately above the boilers. All the arrangements of the ship were admirably fitted to produce discomfort and disgust, which were intensified by the slowness of speed, two days and the intervening night being consumed in traversing the two hundred and ninety miles between the two ports. We kept out to sea far enough to escape any view of the coast. The first land to greet the eye as we approached Hainan were seven small rocky islands, one of them perforated in a peculiar way by a great tunnel. Mu-fu Point, Po-tsin pagoda, and Hainan Head, appear successively as we enter the straits. The latter is the most dangerous point on the route; the rocks and the currents are so treacherous and the channel so intricate, that no ship will go through in the night. These difficulties of the passage are increased by the state of the tides, which ebb and flow through the straits but once in twenty-four hours. Long lines of white spray showed where the breakers were dashing on

---

79   A form of palm tree.

the sandy beach of the peninsula jutting out from the mainland opposite.

Late in the afternoon we dropped anchor in the open roadstead. The disadvantages of the harbour were at once apparent. The town lies three miles distant across a shallow bay, the inner portion showing only a broad stretch of slimy mud at low tide. Access to the town by boat is only possible when the tide is well up. The inconvenience of such a state of things, in the event of the frequent arrival of steamers or the shipment of large cargoes, is easily imagined. Our slow passage brought us there just in time to receive all the discomforts of low water. A fleet of small boats that had been lying in wait around a point hoisted sail as soon as the harbour-master's boat pulled alongside of us, which was to them the signal that passengers were free to land. We took passage in one of these boats, but did not land until nearly midnight, five hours after leaving the ship. The cleanliness and quiet of my friend's cosy quarters were a great relief after the discomfort of the voyage.

Hoi-how has one principal street, along which most of the business is done. The town is rather straggling, having no good centre around which to cluster; a part is enclosed by a wall, and branches extend along the streams. The ten or twelve Europeans who compose the foreign community are stowed away in Chinese houses, and are only found after persistent search. The trade of the port has hardly realised the expectations awakened at its opening. Sugar, oil, and live pigs are the chief exports. Cocoa-nut ware, rattan, leather, and other articles are shipped in smaller quantities. The junk trade, long established at other ports along the coast as well as here, still draws the main bulk of traffic in cocoa-nut, betel nuts, salt, salt fish, hides, and tallow. The principal import trade is done in opium, which comes in legitimately through the European houses, illegitimately through Chinese under foreign names, and by the usual methods of smuggling. The country is flooded with it, and its baneful effects are seen far and wide. All the officials use the drug, and in some places almost the whole male population is addicted to the opium pipe. The people, as we first meet them, seem darker than those about Canton and are not much burdened with surplus energy.

The Hainanese dialect is here spoken in its purity, and those desirous of acquiring it are advised to secure teachers with a good King-shan accent.[80] This dialect, which is spoken over the greater part of the island, is known among the natives as the Ke-wa, the language of the strangers.[81] It is not, however, allied to the Hakka of the mainland. Its nearest affinity seems to be the dialects

---

80 Qiongshan accent.
81 Qionghai dialect.

of Amoy[82], or of the southern part of Formosa.[83] We have in its native designation a constant reminder that the early settlers were exiles, banished from their home lands, to which they ever hoped to return. They were not voluntary colonists, not were they all criminals and outlaws, but the vassals of a despotic government, who, obeying the orders of their emperor, left their homes in the more congenial region about Fu-kien perhaps, to occupy and develop the sparsely-peopled territory south of the sea.[84]

The surroundings of Hoi-how are far from being unattractive. Fine walks on either side of the bay reward the pedestrian. Old monuments of various kinds attract the antiquarian. Game abounds within easy distance; snipe and teal in abundance along the beach; deer, woodcock, and jungle fowl a few miles inland. Toward the west rise the high grounds of Ta-ying-shan, covered with groves of trees, abounding in fresh spring water, and open to the sea breeze throughout the year. This is the prospective location of the residences of the European community, when negotiations for land are brought to a successful issue; and a pleasant and healthful situation it will be. The vegetation is not specially tropical. Bamboo hedges, with the thorny rattan intertwined, line the roads;

---

82   Xiamen.

83   Taiwan.

84   Fujian province.

luxuriant creepers, with large attractive flowers, abound, a magnificent species of *Terminalia*, called by the natives *p'i-p'a*, or guitar tree, so designated from resemblance in shape of its leaves to the half-pear-shaped guitar, which, in its turn, resembles the harp of Pythagoras, from which comes the most euphonious name of harp-tree, is found in limited numbers. Its large, glistening leaves and wide-spread, finely proportioned branches, are very ornamental. A few cocoa-nut palms lift their corrugated columns, crowned with broad, stiff leaves, and clusters of green and yellow fruit, above the lower shrubs, one group of five near the shore being especially conspicuous.

Chief among the objects of interest in this direction is the old Romanist cemetery, which covers a large part of the most attractive and valuable space on the hill.[85] Hundreds of monuments over the graves have the cross plainly cut upon them, and the names of Chinese converts, with all the particulars of age, residence, and position given. The inscriptions on several of the Chinese tombs, as well as the size and shape of the monuments, show them to have been men of high position in the church. Conspicuous among the others are the tombs of three Europeans. One of these was a German, as the Latin inscription shows, who died on October 9th, AD

85   By Romanist, Henry means Roman Catholics. Now often seen as a derogatory term.

1686, after being in Hainan eight years. He was evidently a man of unusual importance, his tomb being much more elaborate than the others. The other two seem to have been Portuguese, who died in 1681. Many of the Chinese tombs bear nearly the same date; and the annals of the Prefecture record a plague of unusual fatality that swept over the island about that time. The existence of such a cemetery, so finely located, with such numbers of tombs of respectable people, certainly indicates that at one time the Romanists had a large following in Hainan. The Chinese records give little or no information in the matter, but tradition says they were high in the favour not only of the people but of the mandarins as well, a Tao-tai being among their converts.[86] It is also claimed that they had a church in the city of King-chow-fu, which has been converted into the present temple of longevity, where the officials now worship on New Year's morn, and the emperor's birthday.[87] Still another place of worship is spoken of called the temple of the cross, which is now used as a heathen temple.

The Mission of the Jesuits is said to have been opened in 1630, and to have been superintended by a success

---

86   An official at the head of the civil and military affairs of a circuit, which consists of two or more *fu*, or territorial departments.

87   King-chow-fu being another name for Qiongshan.

of foreign priests for half a century or more.[88] Their flourishing work was probably overthrown at the time when the Jesuits were suppressed.[89] It is strange, however, that from being so numerous they should have almost wholly disappeared. The number of Romanists now on the north of the island is very small, and of those who now adhere to the faith of Rome, few, if any, are descendants of those who two centuries ago were so numerous; nor have they any very definite knowledge of their predecessors, whose tombs are so conspicuous. The present head of the Romish Mission is trying to obtain possession of the tract of land covered by these tombs, but the Chinese officials are not willing to yield up so fine a possession, even with such self-evident proofs of former right as these monuments show. Could the history of this old church in Hainan be written, it would be one of deep interest to us who, in these later times, are seeking to lay the foundations of that universal Church and kingdom that shall never end. Who will unfold the tale of their coming, their rise, their ascendancy, their day of power and posterity, their decline, their fall, their disappearance? These mute stones, with their significant emblems and meagre inscriptions,

---

88   In 1630 Jesuit priests from Macau built a chapel in Fucheng. The first known Protestant missionary, the aforementioned Jeremiassen, did not arrive until 1881.

89   Which occurred in 1775.

giving hardly more than the bare facts of the existence of those whose remains they cover, tell only too little of the movement of which they are the only visible monuments that remain. No doubt proper records have been kept somewhere, which, if available, would furnish us many facts of great interest. The modern Mission, intended no doubt as a reopening of the old, was begun by French missionaries in 1849. Their reception was not friendly, the first who arrived being so badly beaten by the people that he died from the wounds received.

Three miles west of Hoi-how is the city of King-chow-fu, where the chief officials of the island reside. To reach it is a pleasant walk in the afternoon of an autumn day. Part of the way lies over grave-covered, barren hills, and part between evergreen hedges. Men and women are seen riding on wheelbarrows, whose wood wheels squeak outrageously. Many monumental arches, or rather square gateways, are met with, most of them commemorative of the virtuous lives of ladies, who, through many years of widowhood, remained faithful to the memory of their betrothed or espoused husbands. These structures are conspicuous from their ugliness; no grace or beauty is suggested. They consist of cumbrous stone slabs and pillars, set up in the stiffest manner possible. The wall of King-chow-fu, as we approach it from the north, of ferns, figs, and various creepers. The *Ficus Hanceana* spreads in a most prolific growth over the buttresses, the pale-green fruit hanging like numberless pendants over the side.[90] Beside the government buildings, there is not much to note within the wall. Many open spaces covered with ponds, gardens, and groves of bamboo show that the population is not pressed for room. Outside the West Gate is a busy mart, where most of the business is done. Here the trade in cocoa-nut-ware centres. The manufacture of cups, bowls, tea-services, and other articles from the shell of the cocoa-nut is an industry peculiar to this part of the island. Some of the more delicate specimens show great skill in carving and silvering. The shops and houses are all very low, it being necessary, even for a short man, to stoop under the eaves as he enters the door. Protection against the typhoons, for which the island is noted, is one reason given for this mode of construction. In the city, and along the road thither, are many indications of a past prosperity which the present does not equal. There is a woful[91] lack of enterprise apparent; a stupor caused by opium, perhaps, which paralyses all their energies.

Our preparations for an extended journey through the interior being completed, we set out with our little

---

90   Commonly known as the creeping fig or climbing fig, it is a species of flowering plant in the mulberry family, and native to East Asia.

91   (sic) woeful.

caravan towards the east. Sedan chairs are dispensed with as an expensive luxury, and an impediment to the proper study of the country. A few minutes after starting we pass some curious salt-works, where troughs of sand receive the salt-water from which the salt is made. After successive strainings through the sand, it is boiled in sheds erected for the purpose, and salt of a good colour and saline quality produced. We cross a little high-tide bay in a ferry-boat. Flocks of snipe fly up as we approach the shore, and four or five cranes of great size and attractive plumage rise over our heads. A grove of cacti on the farther side affords a fair protection from the sun to people waiting for the boat. The banks and road-side fields are quite aglow with the reddish-purple periwinkle, which seems indigenous here. Ascending to a higher level, we catch the fine sea breeze, and proceed with comfort to the first halting-place, in front of a temple with two grand trees of the genus *Terminalia* in the foreground. The road thence leads for a time in a winding course through straggling villages with bamboo groves about them, which shut out all views of the surrounding country.

At one of the villages we stop for tiffin, and in the dingy little room where the table is set with refreshments we prepare to make the best of it. When all is ready for us to partake, a sedan chair coming from the opposite direction stops in front of the inn; a well-dressed Chinaman gets out, enters the room where we are sitting, takes his position on the couch at one side, and without a word of apology prepares to smoke his opium. A farmer on the opposite side, who had been deterred by our presence, encouraged by the man in the long tunic, prepares his pipe, and before we are aware of it the sickening fumes of opium are poured upon us from either side. We retreat to the open air, and finish our tiffin under a wretched straw-awning, where the wind blows the black particles of decayed straw in showers us as we eat.

We meet many coolies with salt fish, betel nuts, sucking-pigs, and other products of the island, but are most interested in two men who have stopped on the outskirts of the village. They carry large round baskets with several sections one above the other, each section divided into eight or ten small compartments, with little doors opening on the outside. The chirping of the captives tells us that a well-stocked aviary is passing by. They are mostly brown birds, with a lively, pleasant note, which abound in the interior, and these men, after weeks of work among the hills and mountains inland, are bringing out their own one or two hundred birds, which find a ready market in Hoi-how. We cross a sandy plain with fields of sweet potatoes, pea-nuts, and sugar-cane on either side, and come to a little gulch with peculiar clay sides, worn into odd shapes by the action of water at the time of heavy rains. A short distance thence we reach a rocky hill covered with great black boulders of volcanic origin, from which we descend into a swampy vale, crossed by a good stone bridge, which intersects a lotus pond of unusual dimensions. Mounting the low hill on the farther side, we wind through masses of black, rough, rock-like scoria, some of it built into walls to enclose the fields and gardens, and some used as the material for constructing the low dungeon-like houses of the villages.

Under some fine banyans we stop to rest and gather the villagers about us. Everybody is chewing sugar-cane. The absence of tea, the usual beverage on the mainland, is quickly remarked and severely felt by our Canton coolies. Its substitutes are spring water, congee water, and the juicy sugar-cane. We choose the first, being careful to filter it when any doubts of its purity arise. The Chinese choose the other two, usually beginning with the congee water, and continuing indefinitely at the sugar-cane. A few minutes' conversation reveals the fact that the people of this and many of the surrounding villages speak a peculiar Loi dialect.[92] The origin of this patois is one of the interesting questions that will come up for solution as the history of the people is studied more thoroughly.

92　Loi, and the later mentioned Le, are variants of the Kra-Dai languages spoken across Southern China and Southeast Asia.

The data at present possessed are too meagre to furnish any very definite theory; this much, however, is known, that it is the speech of a particular section of the people, who are evidently distinct from the Chinese, and are also quite different from the Aborigines in the centre of the island. Their dress is somewhat like the Chinese, but in stature, features, and speech they are very unlike them. They are full Chinese subjects, mingle freely in business, intermarry with the Hainanese, eat the same food, live in the same kind of houses, and seem identical with them in many respects, yet they are certainly distinct. The persistence with which they hold to their peculiar dialect is remarkable. Surrounded on every side by Chinese, in constant intercourse with them in many ways, the great majority of them speak only their native Loi; while the tribes of Aborigines in the interior, with much less reason, we should think, speak the Hainanese to a great extent. The most plausible theory as to the origin of these people is that they are the descendants of the Mias-tsz,[93] brought ages ago from the highlands of Kwang-tung and Kwangsi to act as mediators between the Chinese and the wild Les of the interior. A mixture of races has occurred, Chinese blood being added in some measure, and a people differing from all others on the island is the result. The name Loi,

93 Meaning the Miao minority ethnic group of southern China, also found in Myanmar, Thailand, Laos and Vietnam.

by which they are everywhere known, would indicate that they must have, in some way, come into very close union with the Aborigines of the island. They may have absorbed one tribe of the original Les, and adopted their language, or the adoption of the language may have been a conciliatory measure. At present they are quite distinct in physique, language, and customs from any of the Le tribes further south. These tribes, however, differ very much among themselves, so that too much may be made of their dissimilarity. Whether they resemble sufficiently any of the tribes of the Mias-tsz on the mainland to warrant the belief in a common origin or not cannot now be determined. There is a colony of these Lois on Ko-chow in the district of Shek-shing who retain their peculiar speech, and if report can be believed, are not on the most friendly terms with the surrounding population. They are probably an offshoot from those on the north of Hainan. Our interest has been awakened by previous accounts of these people, and as they surrounded us I set to work to collect a vocabulary. The list of words and their approximate sounds secured, and subsequently increased, may be the nucleus of something useful in the future, but is too fragmentary as yet to serve any scientific purpose.

As to the physical features of the north of the island, the chief interest is in its geological formation. The rocks which cover the surface so thickly are evidently of volcanic origin. They are hard and black, in many places filled with cavities caused by bubbles of air in the molten mass from which they came. The source of this volcanic matter was probably in the "Hummocks," two prominent hills to the left of us.[94] Those who have visited them say there is no evidence of their being the craters of extinct volcanoes, but the history of the island records no eruption, so that this immense supply of igneous rocks must have been thrown out from the bosom of these silent hills in prehistoric times. The people have recognised the generous provision of nature, and used these rocks in the construction of their houses, which have a massive but not very cheerful aspect. The thick dark walls and low roofs may suggest much solid comfort, especially in the prospect of frequent typhoons, but are not very pleasing to the eye.

As we continue our journey the road leads between large fields of sugar-cane with pea-nuts interspersed. Everywhere the people are chewing sugar-cane with the utmost energy, the roads, streets, and inn yards being covered with the refuse. Bevies of women and girls are digging up pea-nuts in the fields, and start like frightened birds at our appearance. As evening draws on they gather up their baskets and hooks, and wend their way to the villages, their spirits unsubdued by the long day's work,

94　The "Hummocks" are volcanic peaks not far from Hoi-how in northern Hainan.

if we may judge from the constant chatter and laughing they keep up, and the way they chase each other over the newly upturned fields. They seem a healthy, happy set, which is more than can be said of the men, enchained as they are by their opium habit. Our first day's march, in which we travel seventeen miles, ends at the village of Lung-shan, beside which a little stream, spanned by a stone bridge, finds its way down to the sea. We are welcomed by the more respectable citizens, among whom appears a venerable village elder, an octogenarian who has never seen any of our kind before. The country we have traversed is well cultivated, the soil is good, and the various crops yield a fair increase. The villages are numerous and substantial, and the people most friendly and civil, none of the insulting epithets so common on the mainland being heard. It is unnecessary to dwell upon the discomforts or otherwise of the dark and dingy inn where the first night was spent. It was neither better nor worse than many of its kind, which are the only accommodations afforded to travellers through the island.

Although an early hour was set for starting in the morning, a large proportion of the village gathered to see us off. Our attention was called to two oxen which they said they had slain for us. This was a compliment altogether too overwhelming. We had been previously informed of the beef-eating proclivities of the Hainanese and soon learned that to supply the wants of the market town and six adjacent villages several oxen were killed daily. A pleasant walk of two miles past several prosperous villages brought us to an inlet from the sea running up to the district city of Ching-mai.[95] The air was fresh and wholesome; flocks of birds darted in and out of the hedges; groups of large white storks were flying over the fields, scores of magpies stalked over the mounds, so tame that they would not move until we were within a few feet of them. Taking passage in a small boat, we sailed comfortably up the stream for three miles to our destination. On our right a salt marsh stretched for some distance towards a line of low bluffs, where villages were set with groups of palm trees about them. A bridal procession was crossing the inlet to one of these villages; as they landed the high tide made it necessary for them to wade several rods along the submerged path; the bride's chair, swaying uncomfortably as the coolies slipped on the uncertain way, threatened the fair one so carefully concealed behind the curtains with an involuntary bath. Landing at the stone jetty, we look in vain for the town or any sign of traffic. Ascending the bluff by the path which is almost choked in places by the profusion of vines and shrubs, we come to a square tower, and soon after enter

95   Now Chengmai in northwest Hainan and one of the four official counties of Hainan.

the west gate of this quaint little, old city. It is scarcely a mile in circumference, oval in shape, with a most dilapidated wall, pierced by the three gates east, west, and south. Not more than half the space inside is occupied by the houses, some of the open portions being covered with a perfect jungle. Nature has triumphed over man, and uses the broken walls and ruined houses to support the luxuriant flora; and as if grateful for the help which these ruins give to the innumerable vines that need support, she has covered the whole mass with a wonderful garment of flowering vines, some robust, with large, gorgeous flowers, others of finer texture, with delicate blossoms to correspond. Along the north wall is a long barrier of thorny shrubs, more difficult to pass than the best laid brick and mortar. Toward the east a variety of *Thunbergias* and *Convolvuli* cover the wall near the examination hall. One section is completely concealed for several rods by glistening Rhaphidophorids, whose strong and sinuous growth extends over supports of lower shrubs as well as the battlements of the wall, and whose broad and deeply pinnate leaves spread out like a great cool awning. Not far from these the night-blooming cereus spreads its stiff joints in all the glory of its hundreds of gorgeous flowers, some half decayed, others in bud ready to burst in the evening, while clematis, rattan, and a vine with a bright fruit, in colour and shape like an orange, covered with thorns, hang thickly over the wall and tower above the east gate. A weed-like creeper with yellow flowers covers the whole eastern section of the southern wall. Inside and out the town is a wilderness of luxuriant vegetation. Palms and papayas rise conspicuously above the vines, and red peppers, growing wild in great abundance, vigorous plants six and eight feet high, fill the open spaces among the trees to the east.

On the northern wall is a small structure called the "New Sea-view Tower," from which the surrounding country may be seen to great advantage; a few miles distant to the north stretches the sea; to the south-east rise the Hummocks, and four miles south-west lies a line of low hills called the "Variegated Spring Ridge." All the rest is a dull slightly rolling plain, like a wold or prairie.[96] For miles to the south and west little or no sign of cultivation appears. The rolling plain is covered over with long grass and low shrubs. The country seems capable of cultivation, but the people of the enterprise are lacking. The inhabitants of the town received us with civil indifference. The whole inn was placed at our disposal, so that we were comparatively comfortable. The magistrate ignored our presence, and most of the men seemed more devoted to their opium pipes than to anything

---

96 A wold being a British term for a piece of high, open uncultivated land or moor.

else. The ravages of the drug were evident on every side. Our attention was directed to a notice posted up in a prominent place, to the effect that in passing to and fro through the streets men and women must be careful to keep apart. A rather sluggish stream, coming from the direction of the Hummocks, flows along the south side of the town. It is spanned by two bridges, the lower one of which is rather a fine structure, built just above a fall in the stream, over which the water pours abruptly a distance of fifty or sixty feet. Near the end of the bridge is a remarkable stone pagoda, almost conical in shape, broad at the base, but tapering rapidly to a point.

APPENDIX

LING-NAM: THE ILLUSTRATIONS

Throughout his travels in southern China, BC Henry constantly sketched. These sketches were occasionally published in two of the major missionary-run journals of the region, *The China Review* and *The Chinese Recorder*, where (BC Henry informs us) they were 'received with general favour'. This positive feedback encouraged Henry to include a selection of his own sketches in *LING-NAM*. Henry also used his sketches to illustrate the many public talks he gave in Hong Kong, China, and back in the United States.

The China Review was published in Hong Kong from 1872 to July 1901, a total of twenty-five volumes. The contributors were mostly Sinologists as well as missionary- and diplomat-scholars. For many years, the journal was edited by Nicholas Belfeld Dennys, who was also the editor of the *China Mail*, a non-religious affiliated Hong Kong newspaper. *The China Review* was not directly supported by any particular religious denomination, but was widely read by all the major missionary groups in Hong Kong and Southern China. *The Chinese Recorder and Missionary Journal* was published in one or another form in Shanghai from 1867 until the Japanese occupation of the Shanghai International Settlement in 1941. It was long the leading outlet for the English-language missionary community in China.

The other sketches included in this excerpt from Henry's *LING-NAM* are facsimile reproductions of ink sketches by a 'native artist'. Unfortunately, Henry does not reveal who this, now lost, artist was.

There are also two illustrations rendered as woodcuts – the anonymous *Victoria Harbour, Hong-kong* and *Scene on the Pearl River*. While it is not clear who the original artist was (though it appears to have been a western artist), the woodcut is by the French wood engraver Henri Théophile Hildibrand (1824-1897) who, among other clients, worked for the French publisher Hachette. Both these woodcuts had probably been published elsewhere previously, possibly in the French weekly travel journal *Le Tour du monde, nouveau journal des voyages*, published in Paris by Hachette.

Also available in the *China Revisited* series:

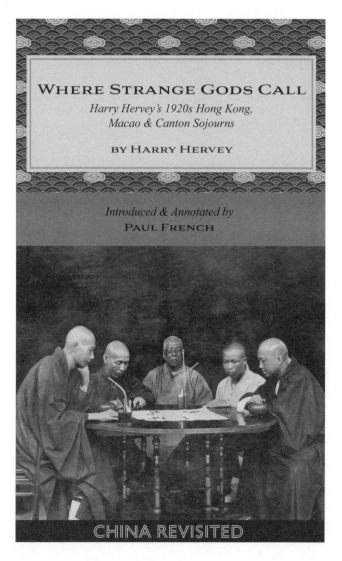

WHERE STRANGE GODS CALL

*Harry Hervey's 1920s Hong Kong,
Macao & Canton Sojourns*

BY HARRY HERVEY

Introduced & Annotated by
PAUL FRENCH

CHINA REVISITED

WANDERINGS IN CHINA

Hong Kong & Canton
Christmas & New Year 1878/1879

by CONSTANCE GORDON-CUMMING

Introduced & Annotated by
PAUL FRENCH

CHINA REVISITED